AI·STA

A Handbook for Entrepreneur, Engineers, Tech leaders, AI Startup business owners and Other IT Professionals

Padmaraj Nidagundi

DEDICATION

If you have ever thought to yourself, "I want to know about AI Startup - Product Design And Development" then this is the perfect book for you. In it, the author comes up with some important themes: starting new AI startups, AI startup ideas, AI for problem solving, AI product idea with a product roadmap, product development in agile era, startups challenges and AI in the year 2030 and so on.

In the book, the author comes up with some important themes:

This book on AI startup provides readers with an in-depth look into the world of Artificial Intelligence (AI) startups. It delves into the successes and challenges faced by AI entrepreneurs, offering insights and best practices for those looking to start their own AI business. It covers topics such as venture capital funding, marketing, customer acquisition, product development, data security, and more. Additionally, the book examines the potential of AI technology to revolutionize industries and create new opportunities.

It also provides an overview of the latest advancements in AI research and its applications in various industries. With its comprehensive coverage, Book on AI startup is an essential read for entrepreneurs, innovators, and business leaders interested in leveraging AI to create innovative products and services. The book end with follow along the journey and self Q&A.

AI STARTUP

CONTENTS

1. HISTORY OF AI STARTUPS

Do you ever wonder how AI Startups came to be? From the early days of artificial intelligence research to the development of cutting-edge AI solutions, this chapter will take you through a brief history of AI Startups. Discover the key players, milestones, and challenges that have shaped the landscape of modern AI.

AI (Artificial Intelligence) is a branch of computer science that deals with creating intelligent machines that can think and act like humans. AI-powered machines are designed to be able to solve problems, recognize patterns and make decisions based on the data they receive. AI technology has become increasingly popular in recent years, with applications ranging from healthcare and automotive to finance and marketing. AI can help automate processes, identify customer needs, generate insights from data, and more. As AI continues to evolve, it promises to revolutionize various industries by providing more efficient solutions for businesses and better experiences for customers.

AI start-ups are companies that develop and use Artificial Intelligence (AI) technologies for various applications. They can range from software development to robotics, and even medical diagnostics. AI is rapidly changing our world and it is becoming increasingly important in many areas, from finance to healthcare. AI start-ups are on the forefront of this revolution and offer exciting opportunities for both investors and employees alike.

AI start-ups often focus on machine learning, data processing, natural language processing, Internet of Things (IoT), robotics, computer vision, speech recognition, and other related fields. These AI Startups utilize big data sets to train their algorithms and create complex models that can help them make better decisions or perform a certain task more accurately than humans can. As such, they need access to massive amounts of data in order to develop their products effectively.

The Early Days of AI Startups

The history of Artificial Intelligence (AI) dates back to antiquity, when myths, stories and dreams of intelligent machines were first imagined. However, it wasn't until the 20th century that AI truly began to take shape. In the 1950s, a handful of scientists and mathematicians began laying the foundation for what AI would become in the modern world.

Since then, AI has rapidly evolved and expanded in scope and application. Investment and interest in AI has boomed in recent decades as technology advances have enabled us to create ever-more powerful algorithms and machines capable of tackling complex tasks with increasing accuracy. In 2021 alone, the amount of capital invested in AI companies almost doubled over 2020 levels to $68 billion.

Today's AI Startups are leveraging these advancements to create innovative products that automate mundane tasks or revolutionize entire industries – from virtual personal assistants like Siri and Alexa making our daily lives easier, to self-driving cars set to revolutionize transportation as we know it. The need for training data is especially acute for these AI Startups as they seek to develop effective products – but lack historical data sets and can benefit from additional investment by venture capitalists (VCs).

AI Startups In The 2000s

The 2000s saw a surge in the use of Artificial Intelligence (AI) in AI Startups. In 1998, Larry Page and Sergey Brin founded the now-legendary Google, pioneering the use of AI in search engines. As technology evolved, so did the capabilities of AI-driven businesses. By the early 2000s, AI had become commonplace in many spheres including data science, machine learning and analytics.

Data was seen as one of the most valuable assets for technology companies and AI Startups alike. This allowed them to leverage their huge datasets to create predictive models with extraordinary accuracy and speed. Many new businesses were created to capitalize on this trend and focus on developing cutting-edge products powered by AI.

At the same time, patent applications for AI software skyrocketed as companies sought protection for their inventions. And venture capitalists began investing heavily into emerging Artificial Intelligence AI Startups based on their potential value propositions.

Today, many of these innovative AI Startups are leading the way in shaping our future world with powerful applications of AI technology that are driving industry revolutions across a multitude of sectors from healthcare to transportation to finance and beyond.

Fig 1. AI Ecosystem

The Rise of Deep Learning has been a pivotal moment in the history of Artificial Intelligence (AI). Deep learning is a form of Machine Learning that uses multiple layers of neural networks to mimic the decision-making processes of the human brain. The technology emerged in the 1950s but it wasn't until the mid-1990s that AI Startups began to make more realistic claims about its potential. Improvements in audio equipment and data bandwidth were essential for deep learning's success, allowing AI developers to take full advantage of the technology and create ever-more powerful applications.

Today, companies are using Deep Learning algorithms to automate ever-increasing streams of data, enabling them to gain a competitive edge and make better decisions than ever before. India is home to over 3,000 deep-tech AI Startups that are experimenting with cutting-edge technologies such as Artificial Intelligence, Machine Learning, Internet Of Things (IoT), Augmented Reality (AR) and Virtual Reality (VR). Causal AI technology is also becoming widely adopted by businesses as it allows them to understand cause and effect without having any coding knowledge.

The Rise of Deep Learning has certainly revolutionized AI development over the past decades, paving the way for even greater advancements in the field.

AI Startups In 2023 And 2024

AI Startups are gaining major traction in the marketplace, with investments predicted to reach over $500 billion by 2024. As a result, more and more AI solutions are being developed for IT sectors, impacting many industries. In 2022 and 2023, AI is set to make a huge impact as numerous AI Startups harness the power of this technology to develop innovative products.

The US-based AI 50 list, produced in partnership with Sequoia Capital, recognizes some of the top AI Startups across North America. AI Startups such as Rytr, Copy AI, OpenAI, SingleStore, Akasa, Edge Impulse and 6sense have all made the list thanks to their innovative products and applications. These companies offer a range of opportunities for those interested in learning about AI and Machine Learning.

There are plenty of reasons why you should consider working for an AI startup in 2022 and 2023. You will gain access to expert panels, presentations and networking opportunities from some of the leading AI professionals around the world. You'll also have the opportunity to be part of something bigger than yourself – developing products that are set to revolutionize the way we live, work and play.

Big Tech's Role In AI Startups

Big tech is increasingly playing a major role in the development of artificial intelligence (AI) AI Startups. Companies like Google, Meta, OpenAI and DeepMind are leading the way when it comes to the acquisition of AI Startups. This trend was kicked off by Larry Page and Sergey Brin in 1998, when they founded the world-renowned language AI startup.

Since then, AI has seen explosive growth and has become an integral part of many businesses. According to research, 50% of companies use artificial intelligence in at least one business function today. As a result, demand for AI solutions from AI Startups has increased significantly.

However, competing with large tech companies isn't easy for small businesses. Big tech companies have more resources at their disposal to develop new technologies and acquire smaller AI Startups that can benefit from their existing infrastructure. For instance, Project Maven is an example of how militaries are using artificial intelligence for autonomous weapons systems – something that only big tech companies have access to due to their size and resources.

In addition to this, blockchain technology is being used by some companies to authenticate content provenance or accuracy of origin information – again something that only larger firms can effectively leverage due to their size.

With the development of technology, robotics and automation have been gaining increasing attention in recent years. Robotics and automation are transforming the way businesses work, allowing them to become more efficient and productive while reducing labor costs. Automation is also reaching more companies, changing the nature of how they operate and impacting jobs and workers. Meanwhile, artificial intelligence (AI) is also becoming increasingly prevalent in robotics solutions, introducing learning capabilities as well as flexibility to machines that can help to improve their performance. As AI and automation continue to grow, investments are flowing in from many different sources for research and development into these areas. This growing interest in robotics and automation is set to continue over the coming years, resulting in major advances for the industry.

In short: AI has been around since the 1950s and has seen a significant resurgence in recent years. In 2017, AI startup acquisitions increased by 44%, with Google alone buying 14 companies. These AI Startups are driving innovation in various sectors, from healthcare to travel. AI is being used to streamline processes, improve customer experience, and reduce costs for businesses. With AI-powered technologies continuing to evolve every day, it's clear that this industry is only going to become more important in the coming years.

2. NEED OF AI STARTUPS

Are you an aspiring entrepreneur looking to break into the tech industry? Are you a business owner looking for ways to keep up with the competition? If so, you've come to the right place. In this chapter, we'll explore the need of AI Startups and how they can help your business grow.

AI is rapidly becoming one of the most sought-after technologies in the global market. It is an umbrella term for a variety of related technologies, including natural language processing, machine learning, and computer vision. AI is being used to automate processes and improve decision-making across industries such as healthcare, finance, retail, logistics, and manufacturing.

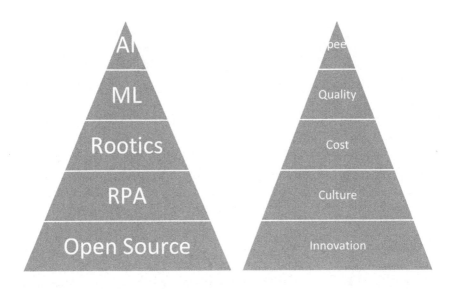

Fig 2. AI Need For Market Trends And Market Needs

The global AI market was valued at $46.9 billion in 2020 and is expected to grow at a compound annual growth rate (CAGR) of 41.5% from 2021 to 2028. The demand for AI solutions has been fueled by increased investments from governments around the world and large tech companies such as Google and Microsoft. These investments have enabled AI Startups to innovate with AI products that optimize various industries such as retail, healthcare and finance.

AI Startups are emerging as specialized providers of innovative solutions aimed at solving specific problems within an industry or organization. They are typically small teams that leverage their insights on big data sets to create tailored algorithms that can help businesses achieve better results without having to spend on expensive resources or technology stacks. AI Startups are also offering cloud-based services that allow customers access to predictive analytics tools without upfront costs or complex deployments associated with traditional software packages.

AI Startups For Problem Solving And New Job Creation

AI Startups are revolutionizing the way businesses and organizations approach problem-solving. With advanced artificial intelligence (AI) technologies, AI Startups are able to quickly identify, analyze and solve problems that would be too complex or time-consuming for humans. They are also capable of uncovering hidden patterns in data that can provide valuable insights and inform effective decision-making.

The most successful AI Startups use a combination of machine learning (ML) and deep learning (DL) algorithms to process data, generate predictions and automate processes. This allows them to tackle complex problems such as fraud detection, customer segmentation and predictive analytics with greater accuracy and speed than ever before. In addition, they can help reduce operational costs while increasing efficiency by automating mundane tasks such as customer service inquiries or inventory management.

AI Startups are creating a wave of new job opportunities and reshaping the workplace. As AI technology continues to evolve, it is opening up opportunities for workers to develop new skills and take on roles that weren't possible before. The World Economic Forum estimates that 97 million new jobs will be created by 2025 due to AI advancements. These new jobs will range from developing algorithms, creating data models, and providing support services for AI products or systems. Additionally, AI can be used to automate some existing jobs, freeing up time and resources so employees can focus on more critical tasks. Companies are also looking to AI Startups to help them build products and services that leverage their AI capabilities. By investing in these AI Startups, companies can gain access to innovative technologies that can help them remain competitive in the market. AI Startups are enabling companies to stay ahead of the curve and create valuable solutions for their customers.

The Benefits Of Investing In AI Startups

Investing in AI Startups can be an incredibly lucrative and rewarding endeavor. As the world continues to become more and more reliant on technology, AI-driven solutions have gained immense traction among consumers and businesses alike. AI Startups offer a promising opportunity for investors seeking to capitalize on the growth of a rapidly emerging industry. By investing in these companies, investors can reap significant rewards as they help to shape the future of AI technology.

The widespread adoption of AI has led to a surge in demand for new products, services, and solutions that leverage its capabilities. As such, venture capital firms are pouring money into AI-focused AI Startups at an unprecedented rate. In 2019 alone, investments into AI Startups skyrocketed by 50%. This influx of cash has enabled many companies to quickly develop sophisticated products and services that can create value for businesses or improve consumer experiences.

The benefits of investing in AI Startups are numerous. For starters, investors stand to benefit from the potential returns generated by their investments as most successful companies tend to experience high valuations once they hit the market or get acquired by larger firms. Additionally, due to their focus on cutting-edge technology and innovation, these companies often have extremely high growth potentials which can make them attractive investments over time

Artificial Intelligence (AI) is rapidly transforming the way businesses of all sizes operate. AI powered solutions are creating new opportunities for AI Startups to scale and compete with larger organizations cost-effectively. AI can help AI Startups reduce time spent on mundane tasks, automate processes, and improve marketing and sales efforts. AI also provides accurate insights into customer needs and wants, enabling AI Startups to create tailored products that meet those needs quickly and efficiently. Additionally, AI-driven solutions can be used to predict the price of materials and shipping, estimate how fast products will be able to reach customers, as well as optimize pricing models for maximum profit margins. By leveraging the power of AI in their operations, AI Startups can reap tremendous rewards in terms of improved efficiency, customer satisfaction, and bottom line growth.

Identifying Companies With High Potential For Investment

AI Startups are becoming increasingly attractive investments for venture capitalists and other investors. By leveraging the power of AI, these AI Startups have the potential to revolutionize industries and create new markets. Identifying companies with high potential for investment requires a well-defined strategy that takes into account a company's current market position, competitive landscape, and long-term growth prospects.

First and foremost, investors should consider whether a company can deliver on its core capabilities in order to meet customer needs. Investors should analyze a startup's technology stack to understand how it will use AI to solve customer problems better than existing solutions. The startup should also demonstrate a clear path towards commercializing its offering, as well as developing plans for scaling up operations over time.

Next, investors should evaluate the competitive landscape and assess whether the startup can differentiate itself from competitors through superior technology or pricing models. Additionally, they should study the company's approach to marketing and customer acquisition in order to determine if it is well-positioned for long-term success in its target market(s).

Finally, investors must consider how their investment fits into the larger AI market and how it could contribute to their portfolio's overall performance over time.

Conclusion: AI Startups are in an advantageous position when compared to larger organizations when it comes to leveraging AI technology. They can build new business processes quickly and cost-effectively, providing a better customer experience which increases their chances of gaining a competitive advantage. Furthermore, the number of deals involving AI Startups has increased significantly over the last five years, with some companies raising as much as $123.7 million in funding. This shows that there is strong demand for AI solutions and that these AI Startups have tremendous potential for growth.

3. THE RISE OF AI STARTUPS

Are you curious about the future of emerging technologies? Have you been keeping an eye on the rise of AI Startups that are shaking up industries with new solutions? If so, this chapter is for you! We'll explore the fascinating world of AI Startups, from their unique business models to their potential to revolutionize entire industries.

In the recent years AI Startups are companies that develop and use AI-enabled products like self-driving cars, chatbots, robots, and computer vision systems. They are driven by the potential of leveraging the power of artificial intelligence to revolutionize the way we interact with technology. With advancements in machine learning algorithms, AI Startups are setting the stage for unprecedented opportunities in data analytics, software development, customer service, automation and more. As such, they are quickly becoming an integral part of our lives—from powering personal assistants to streamlining business processes.

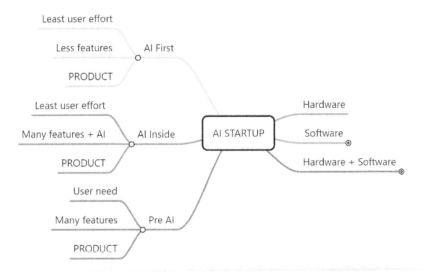

Fig 3. Types Of AI Startups Based On Software And Hardware

AI Startups have experienced tremendous growth over the last few years as investors pour money into them and more industries adopt their products. These businesses have attracted attention from big tech companies such as Google and Microsoft that have formed partnerships with them or acquired them outright. This has helped accelerate innovation in many areas such as healthcare, education and transportation.

The success of AI Startups is largely due to their focus on developing solutions that can make life easier while also being cost-efficient. They are also utilizing cutting-edge technologies like natural language processing (NLP) to create advanced automated customer service platforms that can quickly respond to customer inquiries without human intervention. In addition, they use

The AI startup market is projected to reach a staggering $1.5 trillion by 2030, according to experts. This growth is fueled by an exponential increase in the number of AI Startups, as well as the surging demand for AI-based products and services from industries such as healthcare, finance, and automotive. As businesses around the world increasingly embrace AI technologies, more and more AI Startups are being founded to provide them with innovative solutions.

In addition to this trend, governments have also taken measures to encourage AI adoption. For example, some countries like France have launched initiatives such as PICARD which invest in high potential AI Startups. This has allowed many new companies to enter the market and compete on a global scale.

The next decade will see vast opportunities for growth for these AI Startups due to advances in technology such as deep learning and edge computing. This will enable them to develop more powerful solutions that can provide tangible business value in a wide range of industries including retail, manufacturing, logistics, media & entertainment, security & surveillance and so on. Overall, it is safe

AI's Role In Business

Artificial Intelligence (AI) and Machine Learning (ML) are rapidly transforming business operations, providing accurate, real-time insights into customer needs and wants. Business leaders and investors agree that AI and ML will be essential for future success and growth. Nearly two-thirds of companies currently use AI in some capacity, with this number expected to increase over the next three years. Covid-19 has further highlighted the importance of AI for digital innovation, with AI-native AI Startups flourishing as a result. Companies across all sectors are tapping into AI's potential to drive profits, assess risks and identify opportunities for growth.

As a result of this increased focus on AI, businesses must understand how to best utilize it in order to succeed in the future. From pre-production to post-sales processes, a growing number of companies are taking steps to apply AI technologies to their own operations. With its ability to provide accurate insights about customers, competitors and markets, there is no doubt that Artificial Intelligence will continue to play an important role in business going forward.

AI's Role In Science And Engineering

Artificial Intelligence (AI) has become an integral part of science and engineering, helping to analyze and interpret data more efficiently. AI engineers are leading the way in developing new applications and systems that utilize AI to improve performance and efficiency. AI is also being used to create simulations of real-world objects, known as digital twins, which can be applied to the field of engineering. Furthermore, collaborations across disciplines are growing, with AI playing a key role in making joint working easier.

In the near future, AI will be used to develop novel scientific hypotheses and experiments, creating new engineering design processes with minimal human input. Programmable AI enables and converts AI programming into problem-solving solutions, while Demand-programmable AI helps commercialize and promote AI engineering. With all these developments, it's clear that AI is having a significant impact on science and engineering, allowing for faster innovation and greater accuracy in many areas.

AI's Role Real Life Problem Solving

Artificial intelligence (AI) has revolutionized the way we approach problem-solving in many aspects of our lives. AI algorithms are used to generate insights, make predictions and optimize processes. AI plays an important role in helping us solve complex real-world problems. It can be used to identify patterns and uncover hidden trends which would otherwise take too much effort or time to detect. AI is also instrumental in driving innovation, providing valuable data-driven solutions to existing problems.

In addition, AI can be used for simulations and testing various scenarios, allowing us to better understand the complexity of a situation and its possible outcomes before taking action. By learning from experience and continually adapting, AI algorithms become more intelligent over time and can provide increasingly accurate solutions to real-world problems.

AI's ability to quickly analyze large amounts of data makes it invaluable for decision-making in areas such as healthcare, finance, emergency response, logistics and transportation. For instance, AI can help doctors diagnose diseases faster by analyzing medical images or predicting

how a patient will respond to treatments based on their past history. In business settings, AI can be used to identify customer trends or detect fraudulent activities before they occur.

Overall, the potential of AI is limitless, and it is likely that new applications will be discovered as the technology continues to evolve.

3.1 TRADITIONAL STARTUP VS AI STARTUP

AI Startups have become increasingly popular in recent years due to their potential to revolutionize the way businesses operate. Unlike traditional software AI Startups, AI Startups offer a unique set of advantages such as technical feasibility and scalability, which are critical for success.

AI Startups also require a different approach when it comes to preparing and getting them off the ground, with tools such as data analysis and machine learning being essential for creating successful models. Additionally, members of royal families from Dubai and Abu Dhabi have been investing heavily in AI Startups, showing that this sector is becoming more attractive to investors. The combination of these factors makes AI Startups an ideal choice for many entrepreneurs looking to launch their own business.

The main difference is:

1. Traditional AI Startups generally focus on a specific product or service, while AI Startups are more likely to develop technology that can be applied across multiple industries.

2. AI Startups often require more technical expertise than traditional AI Startups, so they tend to have higher upfront costs.

3. Traditional AI Startups typically rely on existing business models, while AI businesses need to create new ones that are tailored to their technology.

4. AI companies are also more likely to utilize big data and machine learning, which requires a larger team of professionals with specialized skills.

5. Lastly, traditional AI Startups may take longer to become profitable due to market saturation, whereas AI companies have the potential for faster growth due to their disruptive nature.

AI Products and Services

When it comes to AI Startups, there are a wide range of products and services available. From cloud computing services to robotics and automation, these companies are helping to revolutionize the way businesses operate.

One of the most popular AI products is cloud computing services, which provide access to powerful computing resources without the need for dedicated hardware. Amazon Web Services (AWS) is the market leader in cloud computing and offers both consumer-oriented and business-oriented AI products and services.

Robotics is another area where AI Startups have made a huge impact. Companies like CloudMinds manufacture end-to-end software for robots that can be used in a variety of applications such as receptionists or virtual assistants. These robots can automate mundane tasks, freeing up valuable human capital for other tasks.

AI technology has also been used across many industries such as healthcare automation, chatbots, animation, text analysis and generation, cybersecurity, self-driving cars, retail analytics and more. There has been an influx of investments in this sector with many large companies looking for quick acquisitions from early stage AI Startups that offer niche solutions.

3.2 WHAT INVESTORS LOOK FOR IN AI STARTUPS

Investing time and money in AI Startups is becoming increasingly popular, with venture capitalists investing billions of dollars each year. As the technology behind AI continues to grow and evolve, there is a plethora of opportunities for investors to get involved in the market. But before investing, it's important to understand the risks and rewards associated with AI Startups.

You have AI startup in case investors considering an investment in your AI startup, potential investors should look at a number of key factors such as the company's market potential and competitive advantage, the founders' experience and track record, regulatory compliance, product-market fit, customer traction and financial sustainability. Understanding these elements will help investors assess whether or not the startup is likely to be successful long-term.

AI Startups have attracted over $75 billion in venture capital investments since 2012. While deals and dollars invested may have decreased slightly in 2021 due to Covid-19 related economic uncertainty, there are still plenty of opportunities out there for investors willing to take on some risk.

Overall, investing in AI Startups can be highly rewarding if done correctly. Potential investors should do their research thoroughly before committing any money so that they can make informed decisions about which companies are worth backing.

As a AI startup founder you need to note down. First and foremost, investors should consider whether a company can deliver on its core capabilities in order to meet customer needs. Investors should analyze a startup's technology stack to understand how it will use AI to solve customer problems better than existing solutions. The startup should also demonstrate a clear path towards commercializing its offering, as well as developing plans for scaling up operations over time.

Next, investors should evaluate the competitive landscape and assess whether the startup can differentiate itself from competitors through superior technology or pricing models. Additionally, they should study the company's approach to marketing and customer acquisition in order to determine if it is well-positioned for long-term success in its target market(s).

Finally, investors must consider how their investment fits into the larger AI market and how it could contribute to their portfolio's overall performance over time.

3.3 INVESTMENT OPPORTUNITIES IN THE AI INDUSTRY

AI Startups are becoming increasingly attractive investments for venture capitalists and other investors. By leveraging the power of AI, these AI Startups have the potential to revolutionize industries and create new markets. Identifying companies with high potential for investment requires a well-defined strategy that takes into account a company's current market position, competitive landscape, and long-term growth prospects.

Investing in Artificial Intelligence (AI) companies can be highly rewarding, thanks to the immense potential of these innovative technologies. AI has the power to revolutionize industries, enhance customer experience, and create entirely new business models. As a result, investors are presented with numerous opportunities for gaining financial returns from their investments in AI companies.

The AI industry is growing rapidly, and with it comes exciting opportunities for investing. With global venture capital funding of AI Startups falling 31% from the previous quarter to $8.3 billion in the September quarter, now is an ideal time to take advantage of these investment opportunities. AI stocks may be excellent long-term investments due to the potential for exponential growth in the industry over the coming years.

The global artificial intelligence industry is expected to grow from $59.7 billion in 2020 to an estimated $266 billion by 2030, according to a report by Tortoise Intelligence. This has led to a massive increase in investment into AI companies, with worldwide investments rising 115% since 2020. The prevalence of AI and machine learning has also grown significantly with its integration into practically every industry worldwide.

Canaan Partners is one example of a seasoned company innovating in the AI realm and investing heavily into new AI technology companies hitting the market. They are dedicated to helping entrepreneurs create products that solve real-world problems through cutting-edge technologies such as machine learning and artificial intelligence.

The most lucrative areas for investment in AI involve start-ups that use advanced technologies such as machine learning and deep learning to develop products or services that can automate processes or tasks previously done manually. These start-ups often enjoy high levels of funding from venture capitalists, governments, and corporate entities alike.

AI also offers substantial benefits for established financial companies looking to reduce costs and increase efficiency. By investing in AI companies with proven technology solutions, these firms can gain access to enable automation and streamline their operations. Additionally, they can benefit from partnerships with leading AI developers such as IBM which can help them leverage advanced capabilities like natural language processing and deep learning algorithms more quickly than they could build them internally.

Emerging markets are another area where investors may find lucrative opportunities in AI companies due lower cost of entry and increased demand for products or services enabled by the technology. For example, many countries.

First and foremost, investors should consider whether a company can deliver on its core capabilities in order to meet customer needs. Investors should analyze a startup's technology stack to understand how it will use AI to solve customer problems better than existing solutions. The startup should also demonstrate a clear path towards commercializing its offering, as well as developing plans for scaling up operations over time.

Next, investors should evaluate the competitive landscape and assess whether the startup can differentiate itself from competitors through superior technology or pricing models. Additionally, they should study the company's approach to marketing and customer acquisition in order to determine if it is well-positioned for long-term success in its target market(s).

Finally, investors must consider how their investment fits into the larger AI market and how it could contribute to their portfolio's overall performance over time.

3.4 MERGERS AND ACQUISITIONS IN THE AI SPACE

Mergers and acquisitions (M&A) have become an increasingly popular way for companies to gain access to cutting-edge AI technology and talent. In the past five years, there has been a surge in M&A activity in the artificial intelligence (AI) space as tech giants including Google, Microsoft, Apple, and Facebook have all acquired AI Startups. These deals provide insight into the competitive landscape of AI development and the larger technology market.

Research suggests that AI will significantly reduce due diligence time for M&As from months to weeks or even days. This could lead to an increase in M&As as more companies look for ways to gain access to AI technology quickly and cost-effectively. Additionally, these acquisitions are helping Big Tech companies achieve their long-term goals faster by providing them with access to emerging technologies such as computer vision and machine learning models.

The most recent surge of mergers and acquisitions in the AI space has shown that there is tremendous potential for those looking to invest in AI Startups or acquire established companies with advanced technology capabilities. By understanding this trend, both buyers and sellers can take advantage of the opportunities presented by this rapidly growing market.

3.5 GOVERNMENT SUPPORT FOR ARTIFICIAL INTELLIGENCE COMPANIES

The government is investing heavily in Artificial Intelligence (AI) technology, with the National Artificial Intelligence Initiative providing research and development funding for AI researchers. Innovation Fund Denmark and McKinsey & Company have set up a program to support AI-based Small and Medium Enterprises (SMEs). The Obama administration has also outlined an AI strategy to bolster the United States' position in the global race for leadership in AI technologies. Companies such as Defined AI are leveraging public funding to develop innovative AI products and services.

In India, the government has allocated €1.5 billion of public funding to support Artificial Intelligence AI Startups by 2022. They are also providing training data to firms developing AI-enabled products, which are expected to drive economic growth. NITI Aayog established the National Program on Artificial Intelligence and both Central Government and State Governments have committed funds towards it.

Overall, governments across the world are supporting Artificial Intelligence companies with public funding, enabling them to create innovative products that will benefit society as a whole.

3.6 CHALLENGES AND LEGAL IMPLICATIONS OF AI STARTUPS

AI Startups face a myriad of challenges in today's competitive landscape. One of the biggest challenges is attracting and retaining the right talent. This can be especially difficult for AI Startups due to the complexity of the technology involved, as well as a lack of understanding of AI among potential employees. Additionally, sourcing data sets that are pertinent to the project at hand can be costly and time-consuming. Moreover, many companies are reluctant to invest in AI without first assessing its long-term value or impact on their operations. Finally, given that machine learning relies heavily on repetition and iteration, it requires significant resources to achieve results quickly.

To successfully build an AI startup, founders must have both technical expertise and business acumen. They must understand how to leverage data and technologies such as deep learning and natural language processing to create valuable products and services for customers. Furthermore, they need to know how best to monetize these products or services by either selling them directly or through a subscription model. Finally, they should also consider how their product will fit into the existing competitive landscape by examining potential competitors' offerings closely before launching their own product.

One of the biggest challenges faced by AI Startups is securing adequate funding. Due to the high costs of research and development, it can be difficult for AI Startups to attract investors and secure seed capital. Additionally, startup teams often do not have enough experience or domain knowledge in AI technologies, making it difficult for them to obtain investments.

Another challenge faced by AI Startups is determining the right data set. Data sets are crucial for machine learning algorithms and must be carefully chosen for accuracy and quality. Poorly chosen data sets can lead to inaccurate results and poor performance from algorithms, so it's important that AI Startups take their time when selecting appropriate datasets.

In addition, internationalization may be more complicated for emerging markets' AI Startups due to language barriers as well as cultural differences between countries or regions. AI Startups will need a comprehensive understanding of regulations and policies regarding data collection and usage before entering new markets in order ensure compliance with local laws.

Other most common are lack of business acumen, lack of the right talent and resources, lack of trust and patience, computing not as advanced as larger organizations, poor IT infrastructure and insufficient funds.

Business acumen is needed in order to effectively create an AI product or service. Without this knowledge, AI Startups can struggle to develop something that is profitable and successful. Similarly, without access to the right talent or resources such as data scientists or powerful computers, AI Startups may not have the capability to develop their products or services.

Another challenge faced by AI Startups is gaining trust from investors. As AI is still a relatively new field with limited success stories, investors may be hesitant to invest in AI companies due to risk aversion. Additionally, patience is needed when developing an AI system; it can take years for a product or service to become ready for market.

Finally, computing power plays an important role in the development of any kind of AI system; AI Startups may not have access to the same level of computing power as larger organizations do which can slow down development times significantly. Poor IT infrastructure can also present difficulties for many smaller businesses due to limited funds.

Understanding the Legal Implications of AI Startups

The use of Artificial Intelligence and its related technologies is becoming increasingly popular in the business world. However, with the ever-evolving legal landscape, it's important to understand the implications of using AI for AI Startups. In order to ensure compliance with laws and regulations, AI Startups need to consider a variety of factors.

First and foremost, AI Startups should be aware of privacy laws such as GDPR. Companies must make sure that they are collecting, storing and processing data responsibly in order to comply with these regulations. Additionally, they must take steps to protect sensitive personal data from misuse or unauthorized access.

Next, businesses should be aware of patent law when incorporating AI into their products or services. AI can be patented if it meets certain criteria; however, patenting an invention may not always be the best option for a startup. Understanding the differences between copyrighting code and patenting inventions is key to protecting your intellectual property from competitors.

AI Startups should also consider antitrust laws when using AI technologies in their operations or products/services. Anti-competitive practices involve activities that limit competition within a given market which could lead to fines or other penalties if businesses do not comply with antitrust laws. Many countries and organizations are in the early stage of creating new law for use of AI, I suggest you keep eye on local government news.

4. STARTING NEW AI STARTUPS

Starting new AI Startups has become increasingly popular in recent years, due to the potential for great returns and the numerous applications of AI. With private equity investments in AI Startups reaching 12% of global private equity investments in the first half of 2018, it is clear that investors are recognizing the potential of Artificial Intelligence (AI). If so, this chapter is for you! We'll explore the how to start new AI Startup. Many AI Startups are leveraging AI-based solutions to create products that can drive economic growth.

When investing in an AI startup, it is important to consider a few key questions. What data does the company use for training its AI models? How does it communicate its technical depth? Does it have enterprise applications? Are there any futuristic applications involved?

These questions will help you determine if an AI startup is worth investing in. For example, Replikr, a New Zealand startup, uses generative AI to create easy-to-read content and is one of many companies offering enterprise applications using generative AI. Similarly, headlines about futuristic applications of Artificial Intelligence have been incredibly popular amongst AI Startups as well as investors.

Overall, investing in new AI Startups provides great potential for substantial returns and should be considered by anyone looking to make a sound financial decision. By understanding the key questions surrounding these companies and their technology, you can make a more informed investment. make a more informed investment.

4.1 TYPES OF AI STARTUPS

There are four different types of AI category: AI has come a long way over the years and can now be classified into four distinct categories: reactive machines, limited memory machines, theory of mind, and machine learning.

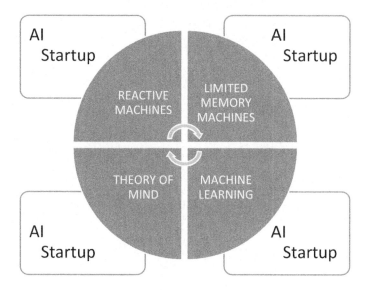

Fig 4. Four Types Of AI Category

- Reactive machines are AI systems that react to external stimuli without having any memory of the past.

- Limited memory machines can remember past experiences and use those memories to inform their decisions in the present moment.

- Theory of mind systems are AI systems that can predict another's mental state by taking into account factors such as beliefs, intentions, emotions, and desires.

- Finally, machine learning is a type of AI system that learns from data it is given and can make predictions based on that knowledge. Each type of AI has its own strengths and weaknesses, and understanding these differences is important for effectively using AI technology.

Most of time AI startup those one of above type of core AI or combination in their business model.

AI Startups are on the rise, with companies like Waymo and Argo AI leading the charge in self-driving technology. But there's more to AI Startups than just autonomous vehicles – a variety of businesses are leveraging artificial intelligence to develop innovative solutions.

Alation is an example of a data catalog that makes it easier for companies to store, organize and access their data. Reverie provides natural language processing services for enterprises, while Walnut Algorithms develops and maintains proprietary data algorithms. Then there's the Toronto Synthetic Intelligence Forum, which is an incubator and accelerator for AI Startups. These are just some of the types of AI Startups out there – as this industry continues to grow, so too will the number of businesses be developing new applications for this revolutionary technology.

AI Startups are on the rise in the tech world, offering a range of innovative solutions for businesses and consumers alike. AI is becoming increasingly powerful, with the potential to revolutionize many industries.

AI technology can be used in various forms – from machine learning algorithms to virtual assistants – and it's being applied in almost every industry imaginable. From healthcare to finance, retail to manufacturing, AI has become an integral part of many companies' operations.

There are several different types of AI Startups out there, each focusing on different aspects of artificial intelligence. Some focus on natural language processing (NLP), while others specialize in computer vision or machine learning (ML). Each type of startup brings its own unique skillset to the table, providing businesses with tailored solutions that can improve customer experiences and operational efficiency.

One popular type of AI startup focuses on NLP technologies such as voice recognition and natural language understanding (NLU). These AI Startups build applications that allow machines to understand human speech and respond accordingly. They also develop systems that can help process large amounts of data quickly, such as those found in customer service centers or medical records departments.

4.2 FINDING FUNDING FOR AI STARTUPS

AI Startups are increasingly in demand as the world moves towards a more automated and advanced future. With investors pouring billions of dollars into the AI space, it is clear that they have seen the potential for big returns. As such, AI Startups need to understand the key insights and trends when seeking funding from investors.

Firstly, it has been observed that investors are steering funds towards AI Startups building accounting software. This is due to the fact that these software programs can streamline processes, save costs and reduce redundancies. Globally, AI-driven accounting software garnered over $2-$5 million in funding range-based average in 2021's third quarter alone.

The main challenge for AI Startups is to prove to investors the scalability of their business model. This means demonstrating how well their products or services can be adapted to meet customer demands while still being profitable. Additionally, they must present an effective roadmap with achievable goals that will help them reach their desired outcomes more quickly and easily than traditional methods.

Moreover, advancements in technology such as natural language processing (NLP) have enabled companies to develop powerful marketing tools powered by artificial intelligence (AI). Austin-based Jasper's AI platform for example generates marketing analysis and provides targeted recommendations based on real-time customer behavior.

In addition, the platform can automatically generate personalized content and send personalized newsletters to customers. The company has developed a data set of more than 100,000 customer profiles that it is using to train its AI marketing tools.

According to Jasper's CEO Paul Clifford, using AI to understand customer behavior and create targeted recommendations is "a key competitive advantage in e-commerce."

Finding funding for an AI startup can be a daunting task, but there are several options to explore. From venture capital to government grants, entrepreneurs and AI Startups should research each option carefully before deciding which one is right for them.

Venture Capital (VCs): VCs provide equity-based funding in exchange for ownership of the company. They're generally interested in AI Startups with high growth potential and a talented team that can execute the business plan.

Angel Investors: Angel investors are high net worth individuals who invest their own money into early-stage companies and usually get more involved than VCs. They often have industry expertise and connections that can help AI Startups succeed.

Government Grants: Government grants are available from local, state, and federal organizations and can be used to fund research or development projects related to AI. These grants can be difficult to obtain, but they're worth researching if you're working on an innovative project.

Crowdfunding Platforms: Crowdfunding platforms like Kickstarter or Indiegogo allow AI Startups to raise small amounts of money from large groups of people online. This type of funding is great for testing out new ideas or products with a low financial risk.

4.3 RISK IN AI STARTUPS

Artificial intelligence (AI) has gained tremendous momentum in recent years, with AI-enabled products driving economic growth and transforming entire industries. As a result, AI-powered AI Startups have become increasingly attractive to venture capitalists (VCs) looking for high risk/high return opportunities. However, investing in AI Startups carries unique risks that must be taken into account when assessing their potential.

Data is essential for developing successful AI-enabled products, but the data used must be of high quality and properly labeled. Poor data can lead to biased results, inaccurate models and unexpected outcomes. Additionally, many organizations are not aware of the legal implications of using certain types of data and may face regulatory issues if these laws are not followed correctly.

Another risk factor to consider is the pace at which an AI startup can deliver results and scale up its operations. Many organizations underestimate the complexity of deploying an AI technology or fail to anticipate how long it will take to develop a viable product or service. This can result in unexpected costs as well as changes in customer expectations as they wait for a product or service to be delivered on time.

The rapid evolution of AI technologies also means that companies must stay ahead of the competition by constantly innovating their products and services.

Companies that want to stay ahead of the competition should consider investing in AI technologies. They should also keep up with the latest advancements in AI in order to keep their products and services up-to-date.

Hardware And Software, Skilled AI Programmers Risk In AI Startup

As businesses increasingly rely on Artificial Intelligence (AI) to automate processes and increase efficiency, the need for skilled AI programmers is on the rise. With the right combination of hardware and software, these professionals can create powerful AI solutions that can revolutionize businesses. However, with any new technology comes a certain degree of risk. For AI Startups investing in AI, it is important to be aware of the potential pitfalls that could arise from relying too heavily on artificial intelligence and automation.

Working with AI requires a comprehensive understanding of technology, process, and people skills. To ensure success, teams should strive to build overlapping skill sets across multiple functions. Additionally, companies must recognize and address any potential employee mistrust towards AI before implementing and integrating it into their systems. By exploring successful AI companies and investing in cutting-edge technologies like machine-learning algorithms, AI Startups investing in AI can minimize risks while maximizing rewards.

Skilled software developers are essential for creating efficient applications and programs that integrate with AI solutions. Meanwhile, software quality assurance analysts and testers ensure the code meets industry standards by identifying problems with design or functionality before they become an issue. With the right blend of hardware, software, people skills, and experience in artificial intelligence development, AI Startups can benefit from the same advantages.

4.4 SUCCESSFUL ARTIFICIAL INTELLIGENCE COMPANIES TODAY

Today's successful Artificial Intelligence startup companies are revolutionizing the way businesses operate. From providing smarter, more efficient customer service to automating tedious and time-consuming tasks, these cutting-edge AI Startups are making it easier for companies to stay competitive in an ever-evolving tech landscape.

OneTrust is a leader in AI-powered solutions for global privacy compliance and data governance. They provide organizations with automated tools to automate their data privacy activities, as well as helping them identify potential risks associated with their data practices.

Amazon, Microsoft, Google, and IBM are all giants when it comes to using AI for business purposes. These companies have developed powerful technologies that can help them better understand customer behavior and develop personalized products and services. In addition, they are also investing heavily in research and development to advance their AI capabilities even further.

Failing to sell artificial intelligence licenses kills AI Startups is a company that helps other businesses market and sell their own artificial intelligence licenses by providing expert advice on how best to do so. This firm helps its clients create marketing plans that make use of the latest technology trends such as machine learning algorithms and natural language processing (NLP).

In conclusion, Artificial Intelligence (AI) is one of the fastest-growing technology that is making human life much easier by automating processes and displacing employees. AI start-ups are redefining industries and have been receiving an increased amount of attention from investors. AI companies are utilizing supervised learning algorithms based on historical data to train their models and make decisions. These algorithms have been used in various fields such as healthcare, finance, and retail. However, early-stage AI start-ups lack necessary funding and resources to compete with well-established firms. To maximize the potential of this technology, more funding should be allocated for AI Startups to ensure their success in the long run.

4.5 AI STARTUP IDEAS

Generating AI startup ideas can be done through various methods. One such method is using the GPT-4 powered startup idea generator by serial maker and Golden Kitty Award Winner, Pieter

Levels, called IdeasAI.

Another way is to analyze the competition, understand their offerings and pricing strategies, and analyze the market for opportunities.

Additionally, it is important to ensure that your idea cannot be achieved without AI in order to develop an effective AI startup. Next steps take some my example for AI startups.

MY AI STARTUP IDEAS

1. AI-Powered Smart Home: An AI-powered home automation system that can control all the appliances, lights, and other devices in the home.

2. AI-Powered Security Systems: An AI powered security system that can detect threats and alert authorities accordingly.

3. AI-driven Smart Homes – Create an AI-powered home automation system that can respond to voice commands and control various components such as lights, heating, cooling, etc.

4. Drone Delivery – Develop an AI-powered drone delivery platform that can deliver items quickly and safely.

5. Smart Healthcare – Create an AI-enabled healthcare system that can provide personalized recommendations and treatments based on patient data.

6. ChatGPT Business Ideas – Develop an AI chatbot platform that can provide customer service, sales advice, and other services to businesses.

7. Energy-Related Startups – Develop an AI-powered energy management system that can provide insights on energy usage and suggest ways to save money on energy bills.

Another best option is a brainstorming session for idea

generation. You can do it alone or with your team to get to know! How AI can solve real-life problems.

There are many potential hardware AI startup ideas that can be explored in 2023.

These include AI-powered email marketing platforms, AI-powered agriculture solutions, AI-powered consulting services, and more. Intel and other big players are investing heavily in AI customized hardware, leaving plenty of room for entrepreneurs and startups to explore new opportunities in the field.

Examples of existing startups include SambaNova Systems, Cerebras Systems, and Accubits.

In addition to developing a great business idea, it is important to assemble a strong team. AI startups need very talented engineers and data scientists. A strong team will help you execute your business idea and tap into new opportunities.

AI startups need to be well-funded in order to thrive. AI startups are expensive to operate and will require significant investment in order to grow. Startups should consider seeking out investors who have a strong interest in AI technology.

AI startups need to have a clear understanding of their target market. Startups should consider conducting market research in order to better understand the needs of their target market. Additionally, startups should consider developing a marketing strategy that will help them reach their target market.AI startups need to have a strong team in order to succeed. Startups should consider hiring individuals with experience in AI technology.

Additionally, startups should consider investing in training for their team members. AI startups need to have a clear understanding of the regulatory environment. Startups should consult with legal counsel to ensure that their operations comply with applicable laws and regulations.AI startups should consider partnering with larger companies in the AI space. These partnerships can provide valuable resources and expertise to help startups grow their businesses.

5. AI FOR PROBLEM SOLVING

Do you want to find innovative solutions to complex problems? Are you looking for ways to streamline your business processes? If so, then look no further! Artificial Intelligence (AI) is a powerful tool that can help you solve all sorts of problems. In this chapter, we'll explore how AI can be used to tackle various challenges and how it can help you improve operations. If so, this chapter is for you! We'll explore that how AI can be used for problem solving.

Artificial Intelligence (AI) is the study of intelligent machines and software, or artificial agents, that are capable of performing tasks traditionally requiring human intelligence. AI enables machines to learn from experience, adjust to new inputs, and perform human-like tasks such as language translation, face recognition, problem solving and decision making. AI technologies can help humans in areas such as healthcare, manufacturing, education and finance by providing valuable insights into data and improving efficiency. AI has also been used in robotics for navigation, manipulation and speech recognition. The goal of AI research is to create algorithms that allow computers to learn from data and solve problems autonomously with minimal human intervention.

AI (Artificial Intelligence) is a branch of computer science that enables machines to perform tasks and solve problems in ways that are similar to humans. AI can learn from data, reason logically, and make decisions based on the information it has been given. It is used in a variety of applications such as robotics, autonomous vehicles, natural language processing, and facial recognition. AI works by analyzing large amounts of data to identify patterns or trends in order to arrive at an answer or conclusion.

The process of AI starts with training the machine on existing data sets so it can learn how to recognize and respond to different situations. This training involves feeding the machine with large amounts of data so it can recognize patterns and gain insights into how it should react to certain scenarios. Once trained, the machine can then be used for various tasks such as recognizing objects in photos or text documents and providing recommendations based on user preferences.

In addition to recognizing patterns in data sets, AI is also able to use its knowledge base to solve complex problems. For example, AI-based systems are often used for medical diagnosis by taking into account a patient's symptoms and medical history before making a diagnosis or recommending a treatment plan. Similarly, financial institutions use AI-driven algorithms for credit scoring by taking into account factors such as income level and debt-to-income ratio before providing financial services like loans or credit cards.

AI is becoming increasingly important in many fields due its ability to quickly analyze vast amounts of data and provide solutions or recommendations faster than humans could ever do manually. By leveraging the power of artificial intelligence, businesses can improve their operations while gaining valuable insights from their data sets which may otherwise have gone unnoticed by humans alone.

5.1 PROBLEM SOLVING USING AI

Problem-solving is an integral part of our lives. It involves using logical reasoning and critical thinking to identify a solution to a problem or challenge we face. Problem-solving can take place on both a personal and professional level, in any given situation.

In Artificial Intelligence (AI), problem-solving refers to researching a solution to complex issues by utilizing algorithms and data analysis techniques, such as machine learning, natural language processing and robotic process automation. AI has the potential to help us solve problems that are too difficult for humans to solve on their own. Additionally, AI can help us process large amounts of data quickly and accurately, allowing us to make more informed decisions faster than ever before.

The problem-solving agent performs precisely by defining problems and several solutions. This is done by building an artificially intelligent system that can solve that particular problem in the most efficient way possible. Examples of this include games like Sudoku being solved by AI systems or robots being used in warehouses to automate processes with greater accuracy and efficiency than humans could achieve on their own.

Instead of trying to construct algorithms to solve problems, AI researchers have concentrated on using the more successful methods used by human experts when solving problems related to decision making or game theory. The ultimate aim of artificial intelligence is to create systems that can solve real-world problems autonomously with little or no human intervention necessary. It does this by employing efficient and logical algorithms, as well as interpreting large amounts of data collected from various sources through machine learning techniques such as deep learning or reinforcement learning.

In next sub chapter, we will discuss the methods for solving real world problems using Artificial Intelligence (AI) techniques such as machine learning, deep learning, natural language.

5.2 BENEFITS OF AI IN PROBLEM SOLVING

Artificial Intelligence (AI) is revolutionizing the way businesses tackle problems. AI can provide insights into data that would have been impossible to uncover through manual efforts. AI-driven problem solving is faster, more accurate and can lead to data-driven decisions that are based on evidence and knowledge rather than guesswork or intuition.

Businesses can leverage AI for automated analyses, predictive models and intelligent recommendations that enable the development of new solutions for complex problems. AI also helps in curating relevant information from multiple sources in order to identify patterns and correlations between variables that may not be apparent at first glance. With all these benefits, it's no wonder why many organizations are now embracing the power of AI as a tool for problem solving.

5.3 TYPES OF AI USED IN PROBLEM SOLVING

Problem solving using Artificial Intelligence (AI) is a process that is becoming increasingly popular in businesses, industries and educational settings. AI can be used to solve complex problems that would otherwise be too difficult or time-consuming for humans to solve alone. AI works by analyzing data, creating models and algorithms that are used to identify patterns, develop insights, and provide solutions. There are several types of AI techniques used to solve various problems, such as search algorithms, genetic algorithms, rule-based systems, neural networks and fuzzy logic.

Search algorithms are one of the most common methods of problem-solving in AI. Search algorithms attempt to find a specific solution from a large set of possible solutions through exploration and backtracking. They can also be used for pathfinding and navigation tasks.

Genetic algorithms use biological processes such as selection and mutation in order to evolve optimal solutions to problems over time. This type of algorithm is often used when many possible combinations need to be tested in order to find the best solution.

Fig 5. Types Of AI Processes

Rule-based systems are another type of problem-solving technique in AI. This involves creating rules or instructions which the system then follows in order to reach its goal state or solution. Rule-based systems can also include decision trees which utilize "if/then" statements allowing the system to decide what action should be taken next based on certain input criteria or conditions being met.

Neural networks are an artificial intelligence technique inspired by biological neurons found in the human brain which allow machines to learn from experience without being explicitly programmed how do so. Neural networks allow machines recognize patterns from data sets as well as make predictions based on those patterns they have learned from previous experiences or data sets provided.

USING MACHINE LEARNING FOR PROBLEM SOLVING

Machine learning is a subset of Artificial Intelligence (AI) that focuses on enabling computers to learn from data and identify patterns. By using machine learning algorithms, computers can be taught to solve complex problems without the need for explicit programming. This has made machine learning an indispensable tool in solving difficult problems across various fields such as healthcare, finance, marketing and robotics. With its ability to process large amounts of data quickly and make accurate predictions, machine learning is used to build smarter systems that can detect anomalies, recognize patterns and automate processes. From automated medical diagnosis systems to autonomous vehicles and predictive analytics tools, machine learning has revolutionized the way we solve problems today.

LEVERAGING DEEP LEARNING FOR PROBLEM SOLVING

Leveraging deep learning for problem solving is an effective way to approach challenging scientific and industrial problems. Deep learning algorithms are able to analyze large amounts of data and uncover patterns that help in solving complex tasks. This technology provides computers with the ability to learn without being explicitly programmed, allowing them to discover new ways of reaching desired outcomes. AI can be applied in various scenarios, such as classification and regression problems or tackling unstructured data sets. It is even able to invent faster algorithms to solve tricky math puzzles or improve computing efficiency. By leveraging deep learning, businesses can get the most out of their data and use AI techniques to make better decisions and solve challenges more efficiently.

NATURAL LANGUAGE PROCESSING AND UNDERSTANDING

Natural Language Processing (NLP) is an exciting technology that is revolutionizing the way machines understand and interact with humans. NLP is a branch of artificial intelligence that enables computers to understand and interpret human language, allowing them to make sense of what we say or write. It combines computer linguistics, rule-based modeling, statistical analysis, machine learning, and deep learning algorithms to give machines the ability to understand complex conversations between humans.

NLP can be used in a variety of ways – from helping people communicate with their voice assistants like Alexa or Siri, to providing natural language search capability on websites or applications. NLP can also be used for text analytics where it can help analyze large amounts of data quickly and accurately. In addition, it can also be used for automatic summarization or sentiment analysis of written content as well as automating customer service inquiries through chatbots.

NLP has already made great strides in improving the accuracy of machine understanding and interpretation of human language. As the technology continues to improve, its potential applications will only grow further – enabling machines to better understand humans and making communication much easier for everyone involved!

ROBOTICS AND AUTONOMOUS AGENTS FOR PROBLEM SOLVING

Robotics and Autonomous Agents can be used to solve a wide range of problems in the fields of AI and CPS. From robotics applications to machine learning, AI agents can help us tackle complex tasks with efficiency and accuracy. By using intelligent algorithms and powerful search strategies, AI agents are able to find optimal solutions for challenging problems. They also enable us to interact with the environment in a more natural way, as they learn from their experiences and decisions.

Autonomous robots can also be used for problem solving by combining various artificial intelligence techniques such as deep learning, reinforcement learning, supervised learning etc. This way robots gain the ability of autonomous decision-making around complex environments in real-time. In addition, by providing an easy-to-use interface between humans and robots, it's possible to make them work collaboratively on a shared goal. Furthermore, the development of robust robotic systems helps reduce human intervention when dealing with safety-critical tasks such as navigation or manipulation.

UTILIZING EXPERT SYSTEMS FOR PROBLEM SOLVING

Expert systems are an important part of Artificial Intelligence (AI) and can be used to solve complex problems. An expert system is a type of AI software that draws upon a knowledge base to provide solutions. This knowledge base can be supplied by experts in the field who add information, or by non-experts who use the system to help them solve complex issues. Expert systems rely on if-then rules which are based on existing knowledge, rather than algorithms or equations.

In order to utilize expert systems effectively, it's important to clearly identify the problem(s) you're trying to solve first. Expert systems are typically built for specific fields and they're designed to address specific areas of expertise. By understanding the problem and using a well-constructed knowledge base, expert systems can provide accurate solutions in a timely manner.

When using expert systems for problem solving, it's important to remember that they take a more limited view of what intelligence is and cannot necessarily handle situations where the environment changes rapidly or is unpredictable. However, when used correctly in well-defined domains with relatively stable environments, expert systems can be highly effective tools for solving complex problems quickly and accurately.

In short: The conclusion of this chapter is that Artificial Intelligence has the potential to completely change how business is done and it affects every sector. AI can present data and recommendations to help inform decisions, however, it cannot replace human judgement or decision-making. Whilst advances in AI are likely to improve its functioning, it will remain a function of human activity and should be used responsibly and with caution. Ultimately, AI is not a silver bullet, but a tool which can be used to solve complex problems when combined with the creativity and intelligence of humans.

5.4 TYPES OF AI STARTUPS

Software AI Startups come in many shapes and sizes. If you're looking to start your own software business, it's important to know the different types of software AI Startups that are available.

Scalable AI Startups Are Those That Can Scale Up Quickly As Demand Increases

They are attractive to investors and have the potential to grow rapidly beyond their industry and competition. To become a scalable firm, it is important to have a system that can adjust and increase production quickly when necessary. Companies need to also keep in mind the six actions that can potentially derail scaling success when helping their new ventures scale up. With the right strategies, AI Startups can be successful at scaling up, raising more money than those that don't focus on scalability.

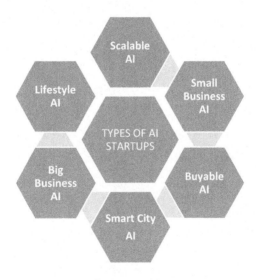

Fig 5.1 Types of AI Startups

Small Business AI Startups Are Those Focused On Providing Services To A Specific Niche Or Industry.

Scalable AI Startups are those that can quickly scale up as demand increases. It's a crucial factor for business growth and success, allowing companies to adjust and increase production levels to meet customer needs. Companies can achieve this by taking quick action on stakeholder feedback, being fearless in their creativity, and constantly striving for innovation. AI Startups that prove they can scale up are more attractive to investors, often raising upwards of 250% more money than those that don't. To ensure scalability, it's important to avoid six common actions that can undermine success. With the right strategies in place, AI Startups have the potential to grow rapidly and acquire a large market share.

Lifestyle AI Startups Create Products Or Services That Enable People To Live More Fulfilling Lives.

If you're looking for a way to live a more fulfilling life, then lifestyle AI Startups may be the answer. These companies create products and services that allow people to experience life in a completely different way. From health and wellness apps that help you stay on track with your fitness goals, to online courses that teach you how to start your own business, these AI Startups have something for everyone. Whether you're looking for an easier way to stay organized or just want to find more meaning in what you do each day, lifestyle AI Startups are here to help. So why not take the plunge and explore the world of lifestyle AI Startups today?

Buyable AI Startups Offer Products Or Services That Make It Easy For Customers To Purchase What They Need.

Buyable AI Startups offer products or services that make it easy for customers to purchase what they need. These companies typically have limited capital but are quick to develop, making them attractive to larger businesses. They often specialize in tech-focused products and services, providing customers with a unique and irreplaceable solution. With good knowledge of market demand, these AI Startups are able to create customer-centric products and services that meet the needs of their target audience. If you're a serial entrepreneur looking to start a business without too much investment, a buyable startup might be the perfect option for you. You can bring on a co-founder or simply keep your team small as you take advantage of existing business phone systems to grow your company quickly. Once you have an established product or service, you can then sell it off to larger companies in the niche for millions of dollars.

Big Business AI Startups Offer Enterprise-Level Solutions For Large Organizations.

Big business AI Startups are revolutionizing the way large organizations run their operations. By offering enterprise-level solutions, these innovative AI Startups are enabling companies to scale up quickly and efficiently. AI Startups are also providing platforms that provide access to the latest technology and tools, giving businesses a competitive edge. Moreover, many start-ups are beginning to collaborate with large enterprises, allowing them to leverage the best of both worlds. Furthermore, accelerators offer a low-risk environment where corporations can source ideas and innovation from startup programs. All of this means companies of all sizes can now benefit from the latest technology and tools without having to invest in expensive hardware or software. With big business AI Startups revolutionizing the way companies operate, you too can gain access to the best enterprise level solutions available.

AI Startups For New Smart City And Their Benefits

Smart city AI can be a great asset to your city. With AI, you can analyze and track how businesses and residents use energy, helping you make decisions on where renewable sources of energy should be used. AI-enabled cameras and sensors also enhance security levels in neighborhoods. Furthermore, AI can help urban planners by studying historical land use and analyzing patterns. Other benefits of smart city AI include more efficient energy, water, and waste management systems. AI also allows cities to use data and knowledge to aid decision-making, with over 30% of smart city applications being enabled by it. Moreover, citizens can use their smartphones as mobile driver's licenses and ID cards with digital credentials. Finally, Intelligent Traffic Management systems can help manage traffic better with data collected from the road networks.

5.4.1 AI FIRST, AI INSIDE AND PRE AI

There are many different types of AI Startups that you can explore. From core AI companies to crowd AI, there is a lot to learn about the artificial intelligence industry. Google, Amazon, Apple and Microsoft are just a few of the major tech companies investing in breakthroughs in artificial intelligence. Abnormal Security, Reverie and Hugging Face are some of the leading horizontal natural language processing (NLP) AI Startups. A business model taxonomy of AI Startups has been developed from a sample of 100 AI Startups and four archetypal business models.

These categories vary and are not mutually exclusive, so take time to explore what each has to offer. Be sure to check out the Top AI Companies 2022: AI 100 cohort for more information on the latest developments in this exciting field.

When it comes to AI Startups, there is an ongoing debate between hardware and software. Both are essential in powering edge AI, but each offers its own advantages and challenges. Hardware companies must build components from scratch, while software AI Startups focus on developing virtual products.

Semiconductor companies are leveraging both hardware and software innovation to create new advances. For example, D-Matrix is creating a collection of chips that move the standard arithmetic functions to the next level. SambaNova is pioneering a new integrated hardware-software system for machine learning and deep learning applications.

No matter which approach you choose for your AI startup, it's important to understand how both hardware and software can work together for maximum efficiency. Investing in both areas is essential for achieving the best possible results from your technology stack.

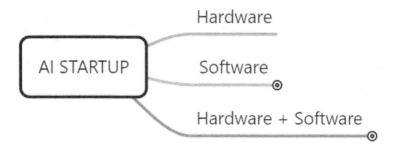

Fig 5.2 AI Startup Possibilities

If you're considering starting an Artificial Intelligence (AI) startup, there are several key questions to ask yourself. How does the startup employ novel or different business models? Do they have access to high-quality proprietary data? What kind of partnerships can be formed? Are there any big tech companies involved?

These are all important considerations when it comes to investing in AI Startups. It's also important to keep in mind that data can be an invaluable asset for AI Startups, and so they must ensure they have the right data in order to train their algorithms. Furthermore, partnerships with companies who may not possess strong AI capabilities can be beneficial too.

For example, virtual scheduling assistant startup X.ai famously used this approach to train its scheduler bot and find the appropriate modes and tones of interaction by partnering with IBM and Dobrin.

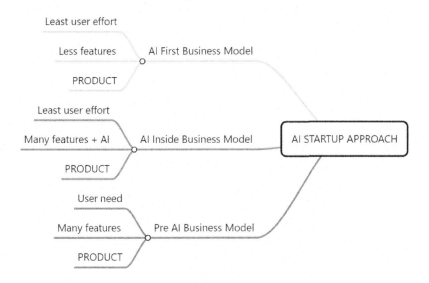

Fig 5.3 AI First, AI Inside and Pre AI

In conclusion, by carefully researching the data available and forming the right start up idea.

5.4.2 AI HARDWARE VS AI SOFTWARE

AI hardware and software development are two distinct but related fields of technology. AI hardware is the physical components that enable AI systems to function, such as processors, memory, and storage. AI software is the code that runs on these components to make them work together. Both are essential for creating successful AI solutions.

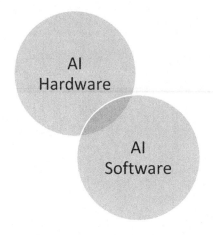

Fig 8. AI Hardware And Software Development

AI hardware development focuses on creating the physical components necessary for an AI system to function. This includes processors, memory, storage, and other components that enable the system to process data and make decisions.

The goal of this type of development is to create a system that can efficiently process large amounts of data in order to make accurate decisions quickly. AI hardware development focuses on creating chips that are specialized for computational workloads associated with deep learning and machine learning. These chips can be used in various devices, including personal computers, laptops, mobile phones, and servers.

AI software development focuses on creating the code that runs on top of the hardware components in order to make them work together. This includes algorithms and programs that allow the system to learn from data and make decisions based on what it has learned. The goal of this type of development is to create a system that can accurately interpret data in order to make decisions that are in the best interest of the user.

There are many different types of AI software development, but some of the most common include:

Machine learning: This is a type of AI that allows the system to learn from data in order to improve its performance over time. This type of development focuses on creating algorithms that can automatically learn from data and improve their performance as more data is processed.

Natural language processing: This type of AI focuses on understanding human language and extracting meaning from it. This area of study deals with developing algorithms that can automatically understand and interpret human language.

Robotics: Robotics is a branch of AI that deals with the design and development of robots. Robotics research focuses on creating robots that can autonomously perform tasks that are difficult or impossible for humans to do.

6. AI PRODUCT IDEA WITH A PRODUCT ROADMAP

This is a chapter I shared the idea of how to create a product roadmap before start planning your startup. If you working in software industry for 3 or 4 years you know already most of topics what I have discussed here.

Creating a successful AI product requires careful thought and planning. You need to consider the customer's needs, how it will stand out from competitors and how to make it accessible and affordable. Once you've identified your AI product idea, you should create a plan for development, testing, marketing and maintenance.

To get started with your own AI product idea, begin by brainstorming solutions that solve customer problems in creative ways.

- Ask yourself what kind of data would be useful for your solution and how it could be collected and processed in an efficient manner.

1. Define the problem and opportunity that solved with AI.

2. Create a product roadmap and identify other resources to help complete the project with advice on what materials you will need, where you should look for experts, good and bad idea sources, etc.

3. Estimate a timeline for your business using SWOT analysis.

- Then look into potential partners or investors who could provide resources and support to help bring your idea to life.

- Finally, develop a business plan that outlines the goals of your project and strategies for achieving those goals.

Let discuss above steps in detail.

Define The Problem And Opportunity:

The problem is the fundamental issue you are trying to solve. The opportunity is the best way to present your solution and show how you can help solve the problem.

Create A Product Roadmap:

This is essentially a roadmap of all your plans, ideas, and solutions at that point in time. It details every element of your business so far as well as your expectations going forward. You may include other necessary documents such as an investor deck or business plan. Identify other resources: With this approach you will look for other people that have created successful product roadmaps and create a network of resources that you can contact.

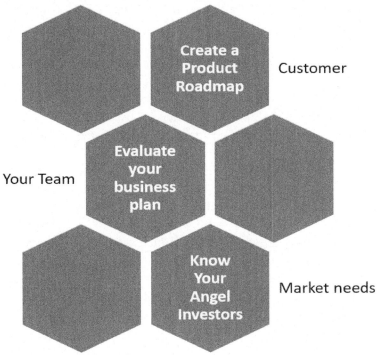

Fig 6. AI Product Roadmap

Good and bad idea sources: There are many websites and books out there on the subject. Here is a list of some things to consider when creating your roadmap.

- Select multiple, different sources. You want to apply critical thinking, so use multiple ideas, but not too many, or they will all end up being similar or redundant.

- Identify the best sources to identify success stories and how they were created. Use them as a guide.

- There will be sources that say "this can't be done", but remember that most ideas are initially received as an inspirational thought, and not much more. Remember it is better to fail quickly and cheap than fail later, at greater cost.

- You must decide if creating the roadmap for your business is worth the time and money in the first place. You should be able to estimate at least a minimum time and money investment before you begin.

- The value of this exercise is to think critically about an idea, look for good sources, save time and money in the process. This way you can test your idea BEFORE creating an entire business around it.

- "Create a product roadmap" is not a bad idea source itself, however it's not very useful without first getting started and creating at least a few drafts of your roadmap.

- Don't try to make a working product before you have an MVP or at least a business plan.

- The best way to test if your idea is worth the time and money is by creating the roadmap first and THEN seeing how much time and money it will take to create.

-You may find you need help from experts in some areas, in which case it's a good idea to ask them how much they charge and their timelines.

- You may need to create a timeline for your business, depending on the problem you are trying to solve.

- Consider all product ideas you have. Eventually, you will have everything from apps to software, physical products, and services.

- Do not only consider your own idea so much as people that might be interested in your idea. Many times I would see an idea and think "that's perfect!", but later on I would be surprised at how many people were also thinking of that same idea.

Estimate a timeline for your business using SWOT analysis: SWOT Analysis – Strengths, weaknesses, opportunities, and threats.

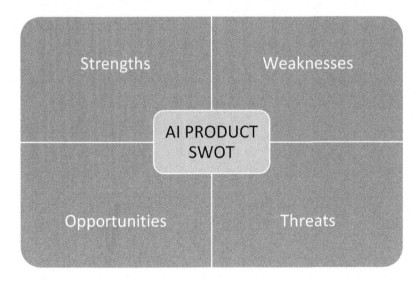

Fig 6.1 SWOT For AI Product

- Create a spreadsheet of the following columns: "Goal", "Opportunity", "Weakness", and "Threat".

- Write down every goal you have. This is more comprehensive than a backlog as this includes short term goals as well.
- Consider all the opportunities to create each product and service

you have on your roadmap.

- Evaluate your weaknesses and write down everything you have to do to create the product.

- Consider the threats associated with creating each product and service. This is the section you'll be adding to most often as you learn more about your opportunity.

- This will help you create a timeline for your business, which will likely be a series of sprints for each product or service created.

- Again, this can't happen until you first create your roadmap. Don't worry, you can always change your roadmap as you go forward.

- Your business plan can also be used for this purpose, however it is more general and products are not detailed.

- Don't forget to include the time and money estimates for creating each product or service.

- You may find yourself needing help from experts in some areas, in which case it's a good idea to ask them how much they charge and their timelines.

Evaluate Your Business Plan:

This must be done, even if you are planning to request seed funding. The business plan you create will be extremely valuable in negotiations and will help you, the CEO, with becoming an expert in your own company.

- There may be areas that require additional plans. Look at those areas and prioritize them based on how important they are. These can include legal matters, advertising, logo design, or servers for example.

Know Your Angel Investors:

Angel investors include individuals who support AI Startups, with the goal of financial gain. They tend to be active in the startup community, and they are willing to fund companies whose products they believe in. They may get involved by providing feedback or organization of events, but they will provide cash up front.

- You need to know the rules and regulations of your state before you begin a fundraising effort.

- Angel investors can be useful because they often have special knowledge that is not available to other people.

- But it's best to have a product roadmap, business plan, and even a prototype before you go in search of angel investors.

- You have to decide how much time and money you're willing to spend on this process. This can include travel, research, and maybe even hiring consultants to help you.

- There are several sites where you can find angel investors such as AngelList and FundersClub.

- Your goal is to try different sources in order to find the one that works best for you.

- You can even reach out to those investors through their blogs or social media platforms.

- Funding is a complex process that has to be right for both parties.

- Be cautious when seeking an angel investor, do your research and you might get lucky.

- If they ask you for something, it's because they want to see something in return.

- Expect this process to take several days, possibly even weeks.

Don't try a single approach and expect instant results.

6.1 REVIEWING AI PRODUCT IDEA WITH A PRODUCT ROADMAP

You're of course wondering why you should trust my opinion on your future product idea. Well, I have a few qualifications that are relevant to the topic of startup reviewing that I think are worth mentioning.

Firstly, I am a member of the Startup Insider Club for AI Startups in the Silicon Valley Area. I have been in the club for around 6 months and I can tell you that it's really helpful. It's like a community where all Startup Insider members can give advice and share their knowledge to help AI Startups succeed. There are also many members who are willing to offer an expert view on AI startup idea development and review opportunities.

I don't know about you my book readers, but I used to be so intimidated by startup reviewing. Even when I read so many AI related books and do the one-to-one meeting with AI founders and case studies about AI companies, I still find it a little tricky to differentiate useful information from the rest of the stuff. Even when reviewing opportunities, there were times where I didn't feel like my review was as helpful as what I was trying to accomplish.

Considering that AI Startups have to work in an extremely competitive environment, one doubts your product idea would become successful even if you spent countless hours doing startup reviewing and research. The reason being is because not all startup ideas are good. Unless you're in a position to profile your customer's needs and troubles (and provide immense value by solving their problems) then I wouldn't recommend you to start up your own.

Which brings me to the next point about startup reviewing - the quality of reviews.

The fact is, not many people are qualified to review your startup idea besides other AI Startups whom have already started up. But that's not all... there are so many people who claim that they understand what works for AI Startups. Some of them even claim that they have more startup experience than others. And in most cases, they're very young - hence don't have much experience. There are also many people who just want to take advantage of the naivety of AI Startups - tricking them into thinking that their idea is good and making a lot of money out of it. By selling them a dream, these people gain from it simply because they know nothing about AI Startups.

These are the typical reasons why I would say 95% of startup ideas are not good.

Which brings us to the third point - the quality of startup ideas.

The decision to start up a failed startup is not so easy because it involves many things. When you decide to start up a startup, you're not just thinking about your financial resources and whether or not you have a great idea. You're also not just thinking about whether your idea is a viable business or if it can be easily executed. You're also thinking about what customers would want. Moreover, you're also thinking about if you have the connections and network of knowledge to make your startup succeed, or if you have enough time to do so.

With all these points in mind, I would like to say that only .001% of startup ideas are not good.

HOW TO REVIEW PRODUCT ROADMAP

1. Look at what the AI market is trending towards

The reason why you should look at what the market is trending towards is because this will provide you with an understanding of what your customers need. You want to look at how they are currently living, and how they would want to live in the future. As a startup it's very important that you build a product that solves a problem. This problem can be a pain-point or something that annoys your customer.

If your customers are already in need of an answer to their question, then there's nothing more to worry about. Consider the problem solved, and build your product accordingly.

For example: When your customers search for a AI vacuum cleaner on Amazon, and the first item that pops up is "AI Vacuum cleaners for Heavy Duties", it means that the market is waiting for a product like this. However, I'm sure you can all imagine that there is a market for this kind of product and you have to find what it is.

Once you have your answer, then you can build your product accordingly.

2. Do you know enough about your customer?

Your customer is the most important aspect of your startup idea. It doesn't matter if there's a growing market trend around your idea, but if no one wants to use it, then it won't help much either. You need to know your target customer because it's going to help you build your product around them.

You have probably heard this a lot: Your customers are not like the others. So, how do you know if you know enough about your customer? The answer is simple; ask them!

Your customers are more than willing to tell you about their needs and problems that they face in their day to day life. If you don't take advantage of this opportunity, then you're missing out big time.

3. Do you have enough money to make your idea happen?

Building a profitable startup is like walking on a tight rope that's about to collapse. You can't fall off, but if you're not careful enough, you might.

Now the fact is that there are many AI Startups which are capable of making money from day one - but this isn't to say that it's always the case. The problem is, most people tend to focus on what they need to do and forget about the resources they need in order for them to achieve their goal. If a startup has more money in their bank account, then they usually tend to take it for granted and they can waste it on things they don't really need. Of course, there will always be the exceptions.

The point is, that the decision of whether your startup idea is good or not, has everything to do with how much money you have available for your business development.

4. Is your product idea big enough?

It's very important to remember that your product is not all the important thing in the world. The reason being is because if you build a great product, but nobody wants to buy it or use it, then it's all for nothing.

A lot of times, AI Startups think that all they have to do is create a working prototype and then sell their product without any further research. Unless you know how to market your startup effectively, this will not even be able to happen.

The truth is, your product doesn't need to be a game changer in order for it to provide a good return. There are so many AI Startups out there which have made millions of dollars without building a revolutionary product.

Your product needs to have one clear purpose; one clear outcome; and a competitive edge (over the competitors).

If you can't answer these questions about your product idea, then it's probably not good enough.

5. Is your team dynamic enough?

When it comes to building a startup, your team is the most

important aspect of your business. It all starts with you, and it ends with you - and in between there are many people who will be working on the product or service that you've created.

How does a business work? It works because everyone who's involved in it plays an essential role. If one of these people decide to leave, then there could be a chain reaction which will spread across your entire business. In other words, it's very important to have a team dynamic that works well together.

A lot of times, AI Startups think that all they have to do is get the right people and then everything will run smoothly - but this just isn't the case. Every single person on your team needs to be committed to the project and understand what their role is in order for you guys to succeed.

It's very important that you find people who are intelligent, who can think straight and who can look at problems in a different perspective.

6. Is your product/business idea for real?

This is a difficult question to answer, but you need to know what the real problem is in your business. For example, one time I was at an event when a fellow entrepreneur pitched about his idea of merging the world of video games and sports. As funny as it might sound, it's quite an innovative idea – so much so that there are already companies out there who have tried it before.

This isn't to say that it's not a good idea, but the problem is that there are already companies out there who have tried building games like this, and it didn't work.

So if your startup idea sounds too good to be true, then it might actually be too good to be true.

Is your business idea going to solve a real problem out there? Then you're in the right direction. The day when you're not solving any problems is the day when your business will go downhill.

So, does your business idea solve a real problem? If it doesn't, then you're in trouble.

7. Is your competitive advantage strong enough?

Another way to ask this question is: Are you better than the others?

I'm sure you're familiar with the phrase " To stand out of the crowd, you must be different ".

Now, of course not every business has to be different. In fact, there are many AI Startups out there which have targeted a specific niche market and they have become so successful because they have found a competitive advantage over their competitors. Some of these competitive advantages include:

1) Better price point – if you can offer a higher quality product at a lower price point, then you'll be ahead of the rest of the pack.

2) Better warranty/support – if you can offer a better guarantee and better support than the rest of the competition, then you'll be in good shape.

3) Better customer service – if you can offer a customer service that's superior to the rest of the competition, then your business will take off.

4) Better AI brand – if your brand is superior to the rest of the competition, then it's likely that people will buy what they see (because they like it).

5) Better AI technology – if your company has invested in better AI technology or better software/development tools, then it's going to be easier for you to make money.

Basically, everything that you do can be used as a competitive advantage over the competition. If your startup idea is strong enough, then this is something you should look into.

8. Is your product scalable?

This point isn't about scaling your business. It's about scaling your product.

One thing that most people don't know is that a lot of businesses have failed because they didn't know how to scale their products or services properly.

In other words, if you're building your business around a product that can't be scaled or duplicated, then your business will fail. This is because it's much harder to sell one product than it is to sell multiple products of the same kind.

Often times, people seek the help of a growth hacker in order to make their startup idea scalable. A growth hacker is someone who knows how to grow their client base by using metrics and data.

The other thing you need to make your startup scalable is a good marketing plan. In fact, if you don't have a marketing team or if you don't know how to market your product, then you're going to miss out on potential clients.

In other words, it's extremely important for your startup idea to be scalable because without it, then you're going to fail.

9. Is your product/business idea being copied?

This is a question that people hate answering. In fact, most people don't even want to think about the possibility of others copying their business idea. I understand that feeling, but you need to be aware of it.

You see, the world is filled with competition - and there are always other people out there who are just like you. Chances are that your startup idea is being copied as we speak by someone else out there.

How can you tell? If there is only one version available, then you probably aren't alone. On the other hand, if people are copying a lot of different ideas, then it's likely that your business idea isn't unique.

Sometimes people are too afraid to ask this question because they think it will bring them bad luck and because they don't want to have their idea copied.

I understand that desire, but you need to be aware of the possibility that someone is going to copy your idea. This is because it will greatly increase your chances of attracting attention from people who are already interested in your business. Believe it or not, some people want to be the first ones to copy a product so that they can make money off of you.

So, can anyone copy your idea? Is your idea unique enough? If it is, then you're in luck. If it's not, then you should look for something that's unique.

In short reviewing the product road map is very important step . When I was in the product development process, it is very important to keep the attention of my product.

If you want to be successful in your business then you must find the right solution for your market, competition and customers. As you see this checklist is the basic one which helps me to define my product and build the first version with a minimum viable product (MVP).

6.2 DETERMINE AI PRODUCT FEASIBILITY

A AI startup is an entrepreneurial venture typically in the form of a new business, which attempts to bring innovation to products or services in order to meet new market demands. AI Startups are founded on product-market fit, meaning that they solve a need in the market and produce an offering that is viable for the consumer.

It's important for any small business to determine feasibility before investing time and capital into developing products or services. The marketplace is littered with new business ventures that were unable to meet market demands, which resulted in a lack of sales and eventually, failure.

AI Startups may be able to save time and money by determining their possibilities early, so let's look at some things you can do to determine the feasibility of your new business idea:

One of the main things you should be doing before releasing a new product or service on the market is conducting minute research into the industry. The purpose of doing this is to identify the current and future opportunities that the market offers; this will enable you to start your startup on a firm footing.

By conducting research, you can start to differentiate your product offering and make an informed decision about whether or not it will be worthwhile investing in further development. If your startup falls short of these goals or fails to launch as planned, this could result in a loss of time, energy and money.

There are many tools available on the internet that can assist you with this aspect of your research, including:

1. Google Trends
2. AI Research Papers
3. Exploding Topics
4. AI Online Communities

Research tools such as these can be an invaluable resource in terms of completing your research and developing business ideas.

When you're conducting research, it's crucial that you find out as much information as possible about your potential competitors and the marketplace in general. If there are any similar products or services on the market, then you need to know what they have to offer and how they are performing.

This information will enable you to create a product or service that is obviously better than any competition that already exists; this is a sure-fire way to gain traction in the marketplace.

How to Assess the Feasibility of a New Product

There are a number of tools that can help you to assess feasibility, including:

- **Market analysis tools** (e.g.: Answer the Public, Think With Google, Spyfu)
- **Product research tools** (e.g.: Helium 10, Exploding Topics, Jungle Scout)
- **Cost analysis tools** (e.g.: actiTIME, Rydoo, Avaza)
- **Business plan analysis tools** (e.g.: SWOT analysis, PEST analysis, MOST analysis)
- **Marketing strategy analysis tools** (e.g.: Google Analytics, MixPanel, The AdWords Performance Grader, Heap Analytics)

The main aim of conducting research into the marketplace is to identify any current or future opportunities that your startup could take advantage of; this will assist in determining if the new business idea is viable or not. The new businesses that succeed are those businesses with a solid business proposition, which deliver value to the target market.

If you avoid spending time and money on a new business idea that is not going to be accepted by the marketplace, then you have less risk of failure. This is applicable to everything from a startup idea to the development of an innovative product or service; this is why conducting market research is so vital at this stage of your startup business planning process.

6.3 ANALYSIS AND RESEARCH OF YOUR PRODUCT IDEA AND RESEARCH OF PRODUCT VIABILITY IN THE MARKET

If you are looking for a way to start a career in the technology field, one of the options might be participating in AI startup research and analysis. This entails conducting an in-depth study on your own idea, product and market penetration. That way, you can avoid wasting time, effort, or resources by entering or investing into a product that is not worth making. You can also know if your idea will fly or if it'll be grounded by working with top-quality experts who are highly skilled in analyzing ideas and businesses.

The first thing you need to do is to do a critical analysis of your idea. Understand the market landscape, design a marketing plan and do specific research on your competitors and the market in order to determine if your product will have any place in the market. Next, create a plan that shows how you intend launch your product. This is going to be vital as it will show potential investors and manufacturers that you have put in crucial thought into your product, and that you are planning it well.

When your product is launched, you need to track your investment, sales and the popularity of the product. This will prove that your decision was correct or not. If it is successful, continuing investing and growing; but if it is under-performing in sales, maybe you should consider dropping it in order to focus on something else instead! So as you can see, startup research and analysis is a vital process for anyone looking to launch their own product. It will show you if your product is viable or not, if it can be a potential hit, or if it'll be a bust! Make sure to invest time and effort into this process so that you can determine the facts about your product and its market potential before doing anything else.

Talk with experts and study their feedback, then use the information gathered to improve on your current plan. After that, go ahead and launch!

What you need to do is to do a critical analysis of your idea. Will your product be something that the market is going to be interested in, or not? You also need to think about what type of product will sell in the market, and if people are going to be interested in purchasing it. The more research you do, the better informed decision you will make when it comes time to act on your plan! In order for your product to succeed, there needs to be a need for it in the market. That way, your product will be something that other people will want to buy.

When it comes time to launch your product, you need to make sure that you are going to have the right marketing plan when doing so. If you don't, then people might not even know about your product. In order for it to be a success, you need to market and advertise it in the best manner possible so that it is highly visible. In addition, you will also need to create a product that is not only attractive to individuals interested in buying it, but also attractive to manufacturers who are going to be interested in making it. This means that you have to find out about the needs of the market and see if your product can fill those needs.

You also need to do a lot of research on potential competitors and their actions, so that you know when they are trying new things out or if they have been attempting similar techniques. This way, you will be able to see what works and what doesn't, making it easier for you to move forward with your own plans for your product. Once you have developed a plan for your product and are ready to launch it, make sure that you have a marketing strategy in place that is as successful as possible. If not, then don't be surprised if people aren't interested in buying your product.

If the reason you are curious about startup research and analysis is simply that you want to know if your idea is viable, then you should not worry about doing so. If you are in doubt about whether or not your idea will be a success, it is okay to ask other people for feedback and find out what they think. Do not only talk to friends and family about your idea, but also talk to people who are experts in the field that you are working in. They can give you helpful insight not only into your idea, but also into their own insights. If you do so, you will have a better picture of the situation and be able to make a decision that is best for your career or business.

You might have a great idea for something new, but that is all it is: an idea. That is why it is important to learn more about your idea before investing any time, effort or money into it. This will help you to see whether or not your product has a place in the market, and if it'll be worth investing any time into developing it. Don't rush into doing anything without knowing for sure that there is a market for your idea! Talking with people who are experts in the field can give you more information about the viability of your product, and help you to develop one that will actually be worth making.

6.4 TURN IDEA TO AI PRODUCT IN THE MOST EFFICIENT, SPEEDY AND COST-EFFECTIVE WAY

Want to have a successful business, but aren't sure where to start? Creating a great idea but not sure how to make it come true? Well, you're in luck. With the help of this post, we'll show you the process of converting an idea into a product that will get you on your way to becoming rich and famous. Whether your idea is for an app or for a business, we can all agree that it's important for entrepreneurship projects to be as cost-effective and efficient as possible. So, today we will talk about the most efficient way to get your idea off the ground.

In order to accomplish this, we've created a list of 6 steps you can use to maximize your efficiency and minimum costs. It's important to do these steps in order, as they all build up on one another. In this chapter, I'll walk you through each step and provide an example of how I applied it myself.

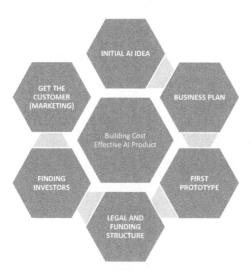

Fig 6.3 Building Cost Effective AI Product

1. THE INITIAL AI IDEA

So, you have an idea for a business or application. The first thing you want to do is to evaluate your idea and make sure it has great potential and market value. There are a few mistakes new entrepreneurs make when they come up with an initial idea: they don't see it through the eyes of their potential customer and they underestimate the amount of time, money and effort required in order to bring it to fruition. Like many other people, I've been there too.

Historically, entrepreneurs have had a tendency to come up with ideas that only make them money. You might ask why so many business ideas are built around generating revenue. Over the years, I've come to realize that most entrepreneurs are driven by two things – money and pride. Many of us want to leave a mark on this world, make money and keep their customers happy at the same time.

The easiest way to keep these diverse motivations in check is to focus on the idea itself, and not just its market value. In order to do this, you need an idea that solves a critical problem in your world. Because the idea is so important, I recommend keeping it simple. Here are a few tips for coming up with a good idea:

Understand your customer - What is the problem you want to solve? Try looking for similar problems in other industries and consult with people who have gone through it.

– What is the problem you want to solve? Try looking for similar problems in other industries and consult with people who have gone through it. Keep it simple - Do not start with a big idea. Start with something small and then scale up as you get more feedback.

- Do not start with a big idea. Start with something small and then scale up as you get more feedback. Validate your idea - Test the idea on your friends, customers, family and other stakeholders. If they are willing to buy it, then you should probably build it.

Of course, not all ideas can be validated. The key to recognize which ones will make you money is to understand your customer and the value they get from your product. Still unsure of how to get started? Well, we've got you covered. Here's a story about how I validated my own idea for a mobile app called Cheeky Checkout.

As you can see, the whole idea behind Cheeky Checkout was simple: to make buying items online faster and more secure. The value of this app is easy to understand - it makes your purchase process much faster than usual. After talking with friends and family, I realized that there weren't many apps like this on the market. I decided to go ahead and build it!

2. THE BUSINESS PLAN

If you've decided to pursue your idea, the next step is to write a business plan. "Wait," you might ask. "What's a business plan?" Well, it's a document that describes how you're going to accomplish your goals. It outlines the purpose of your company, the value it creates for customers and how your company will make money.

Writing a business plan can be intimidating, especially if you've never done it before. However, there are many resources available to help you get started: books, guides and even software such as Lean Plan . They all provide useful templates that can be tailored to your particular project.

Once you've got your business plan all set, the next step is to get it approved. The easiest way to do this is to talk with friends, family and other stakeholders and make sure they support your idea. If you don't feel comfortable talking with them face-to-face, then try sending them an email or setting up a meeting through Skype.

Once you've done that, your business plan is officially approved, and you're ready to make your first step towards actually building your product.

3. FIRST PROTOTYPE

A prototype is a version of the product created in order to test whether or not it solves a problem people are really facing. This can be difficult because you'll have to figure out exactly what problems you're trying to solve for yourself. Honestly, I started building my first prototypes without knowing what I would eventually build – just like many other entrepreneurs.

I decided to start with the feedback I was getting from my friends and family. I knew that the idea had a lot of potential, so it made sense to spend money on putting together a prototype. In fact, I spent over $10,000 in the hopes of making my idea better. This was something I felt I had to do, as it was the cost of testing my idea.

One thing that helped me succeed with prototype creation is the use of other people's feedback. By talking to real customers and by talking to people around me, I found out what kinds of problems the product would solve. The same thing happened when I designed a logo for my business; this helped me validate that my idea was viable and worth pursuing further.

4. LEGAL AND FUNDING STRUCTURE

We've already talked about ideas – now let's talk about the legal and funding structure of your company. You need to do this in order to protect yourself from competition, licensors, intellectual property rights and other hazard that should not be ignored. This step is especially important if you're planning on developing an iPhone application or a website because these companies are sometimes very difficult to crack.

You'll also need to keep in mind the type of business you'll be operating. There are several different kinds of business structures that you can choose from, but you should start with the LLC (Limited Liability Company). This is the legal structure that most AI Startups use.

5. FINDING INVESTORS

Once you've got a prototype completed, it's time to find an investor or two. You should think of this as a component of the funding structure, but from the customer side: if your product is designed to solve their problems, then they should be willing to fund your project. This can appear difficult at first, especially if you don't have any experience with raising money for a startup. But don't let that discourage you because there are many channels for finding investors – such as entrepreneur networking groups and social connections.

The important thing to keep in mind is that investors are not looking to fund your project because they like you. They want a return on their investment, and they will look for it by creating some sort of value or market share.

6. GET THE CUSTOMER (MARKETING)

If you've got your business plan and prototype, you can start working on customer acquisition. This can be challenging since you don't have a product, but the key is to start by finding potential customers instead of just focusing on your new product.

One way you can do this is by using tools like Google Adwords, Facebook and YouTube. You should also think about talking to journalists as well as non-profit organizations that provide grants for AI Startups. This is a great way to fund your project without spending a ton of your own money.

You'll need to be patient as you try to get your product off the ground. Great products take time to develop, and it's not uncommon for AI Startups to spend many years perfecting their product. For example, Apple spent almost 12 years working on the first MacBook Air before it was released. The same thing happened with the first iPhone, which took about two years for Apple engineers and designers to finish.

In short: Building a product is not easy, but it can be extremely rewarding. The key to success is to start small and build your product one step at a time until it's perfected. Ultimately, you'll have a profitable business that will make you and your customers happy.

6.5 BUILDING A PROOF-OF-CONCEPT DESIGN FOR REQUIRED PROTOTYPE

Most people find the process of starting a startup overwhelming. In order to create a proof-of-concept design and verification prototype, it is necessary to know the total procedure that needs to be followed. Here are some helpful steps in this process:

Plan out the project. Figure out what your idea is and how you will go about making it happen, who will be involved in this project, what resources you need to start, and gauge your own skills against those required for the work being done. Write down your plan and think over the execution of it. Write down your plans in a format you are comfortable with this way. This will help you remember important details and coordinate with others involved.

Figure out what your idea is and how you will go about making it happen, who will be involved in this project, what resources you need to start, and gauge your own skills against those required for the work being done. Write down your plan and think over the execution of it. Write down your plans in a format you are comfortable with this way. This will help you remember important details and coordinate with others involved. Your job description – With the job description, you will be able to set out your duties and responsibilities for the project, as well as for yourself during the course of this project.

With the job description, you will be able to set out your duties and responsibilities for the project, as well as for yourself during the course of this project. Resources – Get the resources you will need. You may need to get advanced hardware, software, materials and others. These will be necessary to carry out the project and market it when you are ready.

Get the resources you will need. You may need to get advanced hardware, software, materials and others. These will be necessary to carry out the project and market it when you are ready. Money – It is also important for you to have an idea how much money you will require for your project. This can determine your timeline as well. If you budget for enough money to carry out the project, you will help lessen the risk of failure.

It is also important for you to have an idea how much money you will require for your project. This can determine your timeline as well. If you budget for enough money to carry out the project, you will help lessen the risk of failure. Timeline – The timeline is needed in order to make sure that there are no delays in getting your ideas completed and into full use.

The timeline is needed in order to make sure that there are no delays in getting your ideas completed and into full use. Define the scope – Through this, you can define the requirements being carried out.

Here, you will determine what features will be present and which are excluded so that there is a clear understanding of what format or design you need to have for the project.

Through this, you can define the requirements being carried out. Here, you will determine what features will be present and which are excluded so that there is a clear understanding of what format or design you need to have for the project. Know your limitations – Make sure that you are aware of any limitations you may have and see how that can affect the results of your project. Here, you will either have to adjust accordingly or seek help regarding these limitations.

Make sure that you are aware of any limitations you may have and see how that can affect the results of your project. Here, you will either have to adjust accordingly or seek help regarding these limitations. Conduct a market study – This is needed if you want to define the scope of your product or idea and begin to identify the customers who will be interested in it. All types of potential customers should be identified and categorized in any way that may assist you in differentiating your product from others.

This is needed if you want to define the scope of your product or idea and begin to identify the customers who will be interested in it. All types of potential customers should be identified and categorized in any way that may assist you in differentiating your product from others. Learn what is required for the project – You will need to learn everything about the project. Be aware of all its requirements and limitations, as well as all the potential pitfalls for you to avoid.

You will need to learn everything about the project. Be aware of all its requirements and limitations, as well as all the potential pitfalls for you to avoid. Communicate – You will need to know how you will communicate with the people involved in the project. If there are other team members, you will need to coordinate with them, as well as with your client. It is also a good idea to establish a schedule for all of these people so they can have an idea of what they should expect from you and then be able to plan accordingly.

You will need to know how you will communicate with the people involved in the project. If there are other team members, you will need to coordinate with them, as well as with your client. It is also a good idea to establish a schedule for all of these people so they can have an idea of what they should expect from you and then be able to plan accordingly. Plan for the client – When you know who your client is and what their expectations are from your project, you will be able to plan effectively. You will know who will be involved and what will be present in the final product. You can also establish if there are other tasks that need to be carried out before the project can end.

When you know who your client is and what their expectations are from your project, you will be able to plan effectively. You will know who will be involved and what will be present in the final product. You can also establish if there are other tasks that need to be carried out before the project can end. Establish a budget – You will be able to know how much money you need for your project. This will help both you and your client know what the final cost will be, as well as when it needs to be paid for.

You will be able to know how much money you need for your project. This will help both you and your client know what the final cost will be, as well as when it needs to be paid for. Establish milestones and deliverables – Through this, you can easily determine the step-by-step process of completing the work.

Through this, you can easily determine the step-by-step process of completing the work.

6.6 MINIMIZING THE RISK IN CREATION OF A PRODUCT

There are three steps you can take right now to keep your startup safe.

1. Keep an eye on cash flow to avoid bankruptcy if revenue falls.
2. Maintain a diverse knowledge base to be able to pivot in the event of an emergency
3. Get good at doing PR, which will help when you're ready for the big time!

The key to a successful startup is always to minimize risk.

But how can a startup minimize risk? Here are four ideas that show promise:

1. First, you need to set priorities, which means regularly making small improvements in your business model. To be successful you need to constantly improve your product, your sales and marketing methods, and your relationships with partners and customers.

2. Second, you need to be able to pivot, or change direction quickly and easily when necessary. You have to be flexible enough to adjust your product, approach and strategy in response to changes in the market or new opportunities. This will help you develop a startup that is resilient and robust enough to survive any disaster that threatens its existence.

3. Thirdly, don't be afraid of failure; embrace it! A good business doesn't fail often but when it does it learns from the failure and becomes better for the experience. You can learn valuable lessons from every crash and burn , so don't be afraid to fail.

4. Finally, you need to develop a PR plan that will allow you to go viral with your startup when you're ready to go big!

These four steps taken together will help you stay safe as long as possible. At the same time, they will also help develop a strong foundation for your startup that is strong enough to weather any crisis or setback that comes your way.

In the end, the only thing you can't control is the risk your business takes, so you have to stay alert and prepare yourself for surprises that could put your startup at risk.

After all, some things have already happened that could make a startup as suddenly unprofitable as it profitable. The key is to be prepared for such surprises and stay ahead of such events by anticipating them before they happen.

This way you will be able to protect your startup by anticipating and acting on any surprise that may arise and thus keep it safe from harm.

6.7 ENHANCE YOUR EXISTING PRODUCT FOR MARKET FIT

Product success is primarily determined by the customers' wants and needs, which need to be satisfied for a product to succeed. The market-fit process includes gathering customer feedback and understanding what customers value about products. This form of research helps identify unmet customer needs and validate the idea with target customers, which can lead to a higher probability of commercial success.

Market-fit is about knowing your target customers and ensuring your product fits their needs. Market-fit is about validating that your idea is aligned with the market's value proposition, positioning and business model.

An understanding of market-fit requires that AI Startups define their target market and set expectations on how to understand the problems they're solving in relation to how it satisfies customer wants or needs. Once this is established, AI Startups can then gather feedback from their potential customers to understand if they have a viable business idea.

AI Startups need to define metrics to measure customer satisfaction and improvement over time. They also need to measure important business metrics that are relevant to their startup idea or startup business model. For example, measuring the number of customer complaints or negative feedback is one way of understanding customer satisfaction levels. Startup founders should understand that the market-fit process is about validating the fundamental concept of a business idea. Market-fit is not about proving that your startup will be profitable or generate substantial revenue.

Investors are looking for market-fit because it demonstrates an early validation of whether a startup has a viable business model and its potential impact on the market. It is advisable for AI Startups to focus on key metrics that are important to understanding their potential customers' feedback and satisfaction levels.

The startup market is tough, and there are many product ideas that do not make it. What factors make a product idea successful? Startup founders need to define the metrics they will use to measure success according to their company's own needs. Marketing research can help AI Startups understand how customers are evaluating products and how different segments of the market value different aspects of their products.

Startup founders should create a wish list of customer requirements and review them on a regular basis. They can then go out and do the necessary research to validate those requirements. Once validated, they provide the startup founders with crucial market-fit data needed to develop a successful business idea. This will also allow them to uncover latent customer needs or unmet customer desires that market research has not yet discovered.

AI Startups need a minimum viable product (MVP) stage where they learn about their customers' needs and preferences. They should focus on validation and learning from the market. This means they will be seeking out and listening to the market's signal.

Market research is helpful when identifying customer needs and unmet desires, choosing a target market, validating product ideas, understanding new product opportunities, understanding competitors and developing a unique value proposition. Market research helps startup founders learn about their customers early on in their business idea development phase and identify the problems their startup businesses are trying to solve.

AI Startups can use marketing research data to create opportunities for growth and innovation. Market research helps them determine how they will provide solutions and how they can differentiate their ideas from the competition. They can use this information to develop effective business strategies and tactics.

Marketing research provides AI Startups with a set of tools that help them define their target market, evaluate customer needs, understand competitor products, acquire key insights into new opportunities for growth and innovation, validate their business model hypotheses, improve their businesses' performance and enhance their products for the market.

Market research is helpful in identifying customer behavior, reaching the right customers with the right message, understanding and developing a market position and understanding how to manage customer relationships. It is also helpful in determining whether a product meets customer needs and expectations, which can lead to higher commercial success.

When AI Startups gather data through market research, they can select the appropriate audience within their targeted customers; this allows them to tailor their messaging and pitch information based on what they have learned.

When it comes to market-fit, AI Startups can use primary or secondary research. Secondary data is information available from internal or external sources such as datasets, market surveys, recorded data, company reports, trade associations and analysts. Primary research , on the other hand, is gathered by startup founders through survey and interview methods which provide them with actual feedback from customers. Secondary research allows AI Startups to save time and money in their market-study process because it provides them with real insights into the market value of their product ideas.

In addition to validating market-fit and market opportunity, AI Startups can use marketing research to develop their positions and define key milestones. They can also use it to test their marketing campaigns and communication material in order to increase the effectiveness of their marketing messages.

When AI Startups start validating their business ideas, they will need information that supports the validity of their business idea. Market research provides that information because it is based on real customer feedback which helps them understand what customers want from products or services. It allows them to define the value of their business idea in the market.

Marketing research can help startup founders understand how customers are evaluating products and how different segments of the market value different aspects of their products. This information can be used to refine or improve a product or service offering by providing relevant data on customer preferences, needs and expectations. Market research provides AI Startups with tangible data that can be used to communicate how a certain product will benefit potential customers.

Startup founders can use market research data to validate their business idea and determine what customers want from the product or service they are offering. If their product meets those expectations, it will therefore have a strong shot at becoming a successful business.

Customer research helps AI Startups understand how customers are evaluating products and how different segments of the market value different aspects of their products. It helps them understand what consumers want from products and services as well as provides them with an understanding of customer preferences and needs.

AI Startups can use marketing research data to create opportunities for growth and innovation. They can use it to develop effective business strategies and tactics. They can also refine their products or services based on customer feedback, which will help them determine whether the product will meet customer needs.

Marketing research provides AI Startups with a set of tools that help them define their target market, evaluate customer needs, understand competitor products and acquire key insights into new opportunities for growth and innovation. It provides AI Startups with the information they need to create opportunities for growth and innovation. Market research is useful in identifying customer behavior, reaching the right customers with the right message, understanding and developing a market position and understanding how to manage customer relationships. Market research helps AI Startups develop effective business strategies.

In this chapter, I discussed well-known topics in detail. In the next chapter, I wish to discuss with you the AI product development framework and its execution.

7. AI PRODUCT DEVELOPMENT IN AGILE ERA

AI product development in agile era is very competitive and requires a lot of technical, management and training skills. This chapter is all about the software product development in agile era and how it has changed with time.

The author talks about what is agile era, how it has changed, some of its benefits and an example to portray a point on a right way to approach workforce management in this competitive era. Agile software development principles provide a framework for developing applications while balancing business needs, technical concerns, customer expectations and team cohesion. Agile software development has been in existence for quite a long time but it is only in the past few years that it is gaining popularity.

Agile software development requires the team to work together to create solutions and everyone needs to work in a coordinated fashion. In other words, agile software development requires that people work together as a team and everyone needs to be committed towards successful product delivery. To achieve this, each person on the team must have some knowledge of every other member on the team.

On the other hand, senior managers and project leaders also need to learn how to manage their people and how to delegate authority. People form an organization serve a common purpose and are expected to work together in harmony. Organizations are structured with various departments and each department has specific job roles. Team leaders need a system which facilitates the smooth flow of information among team members, organizations, and their management. Without this coordination the team may fail to achieve the desired results or deliver on time.

In agile software development, there is a lot of emphasis on getting things done in an efficient manner. Communication and interaction between team members plays a vital role in the success of agile software development. The resulting work has to be useful and relevant to its intended users. There has been abundance of research on product development so as to improve its efficiency and effectiveness. Agile product development focuses on enhancing the capability of the team, instead of focusing on individual capabilities. This is one key feature that differentiates it from other forms of project management.

Agile product development is often seen as one of the most effective ways to develop AI software. This has been observed as a key factor in software companies' ability to deliver modern, coherent and more customer-oriented products in a short period of time.

There are many reasons that make agile software development successful:

As a software developer, I have seen first-hand how the successful implementation of Agile methodology can transform software development projects. Agile provides many advantages that contribute to its success, such as improved project quality, faster product delivery, and increased flexibility. Agile also focuses on building projects around motivated individuals who are given the support and environment they need to get the job done. Additionally, there are three key elements of the development lifecycle that benefit from Agile: Initial Project Assessment and Planning, Quality Project Management, and Quality Assurance.

Agile methodology is an ideal choice for developers who want to increase the efficiency and success of their projects. With Agile, the list of requirements can be streamlined so that delays in development are minimized. Furthermore, Agile helps managers have greater control over their projects while also making their job easier. Finally, by investing in leadership and understanding roles within teams, Agile makes it easier for teams to collaborate effectively so that they can deliver high-quality products quickly and efficiently.

The lean startup movement is founded on the idea that new business idea can be created with little initial expenditure and resources, whilst still being efficient and profitable - thus validating their ideas with the market. The more conventional business model would involve extensive research and development and possible loss of shareholder's funds.

7.1 DOUBLE DIAMOND FRAMEWORK AI PRODUCT INNOVATION

As a professional designer, I have used the Double Diamond design model to guide my work on various projects. The Double Diamond is an effective approach that has four distinct stages: Discovery, Definition, Development and Delivery.

The Discovery stage involves immersing myself in the problem I am trying to solve. This requires in-depth research into the subject area and understanding of who it will affect. Then, in the Definition stage, I create a vision of the solution that addresses my research findings.

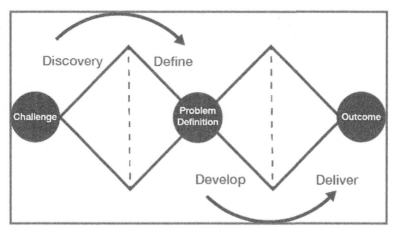

Fig 6. Double Diamond Framework Overview

The Development stage is where I bring my vision to life. Here, I draw on the knowledge and experience gained from previous stages to develop prototypes and refine them through user testing and feedback. Finally, in the Delivery stage, I translate my designs into tangible outcomes that are ready for launch.

The Double Diamond model has enabled me to deliver innovative solutions that meet user needs as well as business goals. It is a simple yet powerful approach that helps ensure successful outcomes for all stakeholders involved.

DOUBLE DIAMOND FRAMEWORK FOR AI PRODUCT INNOVATION

As a professional in AI product innovation, I have come to appreciate the Double Diamond framework as an effective way of managing the research and design phases of my projects. This framework encourages divergent and convergent thinking, which helps me to decide on the right methods and activities for tackling any problem or opportunity. The model also scales well and can assist with transforming ideas into something that can be implemented.

The Double Diamond design model is a visual aid that helps me understand the four stages of Design Thinking. The diamond shape is used to represent the two divergent stages (Discover & Define) and two convergent stages (Develop & Deliver). Each stage has its own objectives, such as connecting with others to create value in the network stage.

Design is becoming increasingly important as a strategic driver of innovation, particularly when it comes to sociotechnical system innovation. Tomiyama et AI paper outlines how this process works by measuring customer value and collecting user data. It also provides details on how this process applies to the development of new wearable orientation guidance devices for blind and visually impaired people.

Overall, I find that the Double Diamond framework provides an effective way for me to manage my AI product innovation projects The framework helps to ensure that all key stakeholders are kept in the loop and that everyone understands the goals of the project. Additionally, the framework helps to ensure that the project stays on track and that risks are identified and mitigated.

7.2 AI PRODUCT EXECUTION

Once you've identified the problem and established a plan for how to solve it, the next step is to begin building the solution. To ensure success, it's important to start small and focus on the basics. This will help you prioritize your efforts and make sure that the initial solution meets user needs. As you continue to refine and build upon your solution, you can keep an eye on the long-term goal of creating a comprehensive solution that addresses all user needs.

It is also important to use data-driven insights whenever possible when building solutions. By doing so, you will be able to ensure that each feature or improvement has been thoroughly tested and validated before being implemented. Additionally, using data can help identify any potential issues or areas of improvement that may have been missed during the design process.

Finally, it's essential to continuously evaluate your progress as you build out your solution. Doing so will help ensure that not only are user needs being met but also that any changes or improvements made along the way are in line with overall goals and objectives. Regularly checking in with stakeholders throughout this process will provide valuable feedback on whether or not progress is being made as planned.

1. Start Small Steps With AI

Starting small is the key to increasing my chances of success when it comes to AI solutions. This means that I must have the discipline to not take on large and complex AI problems that I may not be able to solve. Instead, I should focus on smaller and achievable goals that can help me build confidence and momentum.

To do this, I need a well-structured plan that outlines what steps I should take and how much resources I need in order to achieve my goals. It is also important to get input from other members of the team so that we can more accurately estimate costs and allocate resources accordingly.

Additionally, it is important for all stakeholders - such as owners, architects, engineers, contractors - to understand the limitations of their roles and responsibilities in order to avoid conflicts in the future. To ensure success, it is best practice to avoid taking unnecessary risks or chances unless absolutely necessary.

Finally, there are many tools available now such as TeamAmp which are part of AI Assurance Suitesthat offer projects the ability to increase their odds of success by providing accurate insights into their project goals. All these strategies can help me structure a solution for success when working with AI solutions.

2: Augmentation Versus Automation To Make Better Decisions Faster

With the rise of Artificial Intelligence (AI), automation has become a popular term. Automation refers to the ability to delegate repetitive or undesirable tasks that were previously done manually to computers. AI is synonymous with automation because it gives users the power to offload manual tasks to machines in order to save time and energy.

AI should be used as a tool for augmentation rather than full automation. Augmentation involves using AI in combination with human knowledge, allowing us to make better decisions faster while still using our expertise on complex problems. The impact of AI is clear: it can automate some tedious and mundane tasks while freeing up humans for more creative activities that require higher-level thinking skills.

Note from my side: When it comes to automation and augmentation, it's important to weigh the cost of false positives and false negatives. The implications of such errors can be extremely high, particularly when human safety is at risk. False negatives can lead to an unnecessary amount of time and effort being wasted on a reported problem that does not exist in reality.

Artificial Intelligence (AI) is already helping radiologists reduce their false positive rates by 37.3% and requested biopsies by 27.8%, while maintaining accuracy. AI can also help reduce false negative errors, especially for rare classes; this reduces the impact they have on contrastive data analysis. Additionally, augmented AI is an adjunct to human intelligence and does not replace it; it increases actual false-positive rates while providing flexibility in data collection, analysis, and reporting.

Ultimately, researchers need to be aware of the estimated and accepted rates of both false positives and false negatives in order to avoid setting extremely high-performance expectations that could further increase these rates unnecessarily.

7.3 LEAN APPROACH IN EACH STAGE

A lean approach to AI product development is an approach to software product development that values minimizing the time it takes to create a new product while maximizing value delivered by the resulting product. Lean products are usually developed with collaboration and to make sure they are always adding value. The lean approach is relatively different from traditional approaches, especially in its focus on collaboration, which usually relies on more agile methods like Scrum or wikis. The quick pace of the agile approach may in some cases result in less time spent on understanding the problem that needs to be solved.

The lean approach to AI product development was developed during a consulting engagement with one of our clients, to improve their software development processes and make them more efficient. We used this experience as a springboard to develop the Lean approach, which we have since used as an internal policy for creating new products for our own clients.

The lean approach is focused on:

The most important part of the Lean approach is its emphasis on collaborating. The core idea of it is to make sure that the people involved in creating a product are all working towards the same goal and understand what they are doing and why they are doing it. This allows anyone to ask questions or challenge any decisions, which in turn helps create a better product and lower risk of failure.

At its core, the lean approach to software development is a set of principles that were developed during a consulting engagement between two of our team members, both of whom are software engineers. We used this experience as a springboard to develop the Lean approach, which we have since used as an internal policy for creating new products for our own clients.

But why do we need an approach at all? Everyone has their own way of doing things and everyone wants to be successful in their field; some ways may be better than others. The Lean approach was developed during a consulting engagement with one of our clients, to improve their software development processes and make them more efficient. We used this experience as a springboard to develop the Lean approach, which we have since used as an internal policy for creating new products for our own clients.

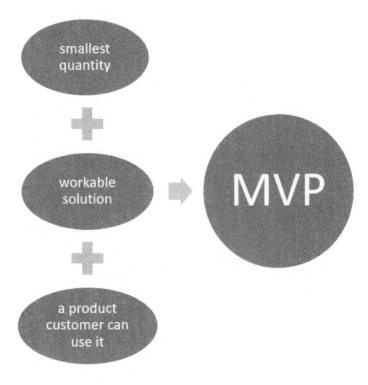

Fig 6.1 Building minimum viable AI product (MVP)

The main idea behind the Lean approach is that the best way of doing anything is to collaborate and work together. So it makes sense to use tools and methodologies that make sure everyone is working towards the same goal at all times. By collaborating, we are better able to see what is being done and where work needs to be done so that we can improve our products. That's why the Lean approach places a strong emphasis on collaboration, which usually relies on more agile methods like Scrum or wikis. The quick pace of the agile approach may in some cases result in less time spent on understanding the problem that needs to be solved.

Lean also takes into account changing business requirements and is therefore a good way of establishing a baseline for future product releases. By collaborating, it's possible to work out issues early so they don't become problems later on. It allows flexibility and adaptivity and by keeping things simple, it makes sure that the best solution is used instead of focusing too much on technical details.

The lean approach is flexible and adaptable, constantly evolving with changing needs or requirements.

The main idea behind the Lean approach is that the best way of doing anything is to collaborate and work together. So it makes sense to use tools and methodologies that make sure everyone is working towards the same goal at all times. By collaborating, we are better able to see what is being done and where work needs to be done so that we can improve our products.

That's why the Lean approach places a strong emphasis on collaboration, which usually relies on more agile methods like Scrum or wikis. The quick pace of the agile approach may in some cases result in less time spent on understanding the problem that needs to be solved.

This is how we ended up with our methodologies and tools, which we have since used as an internal policy for creating new products. We call it the Lean approach to software product development and we will explain it by using an example below.

Lean starts with the problem. What is it that we want to accomplish, what kind of software do we need? This is a very important step because it's easy to get distracted and end up with a product that sort of accomplishes what you want but in a very different way than imagined. When this happens, you have created something that is cool in its own right but is not ideal for what you set out to do. So start by figuring out exactly what you need and then move on to step number two: defining your needs.

As a software developer or business owners, you will always have to be looking for more efficient ways of doing things. If your toolset is not up to date, you will have to keep updating it at all times and that can be costly and time consuming. The lean approach take this into account by starting with identifying the critical functions that your application needs and then creating the minimum viable product (MVP).

An MVP is a simple product or prototype that offers the most basic coverage of features and functionalities that are desired by the client. This gives the client a chance to view and test the product, allowing for changes in accordance with their needs.

The MVP is just a starting point, not the solution you eventually want to take forward. It gives everyone involved in the production of your product an opportunity to think about what you want and what you can do with it. Having everyone involved from the start of a project makes collaboration easier, allowing problems to be discovered earlier rather than later on. It also allows a more flexible approach.

Once the MVP is ready, take it to your client and get their feedback. Most clients like to see what you have created as an early warning. This gives them a chance to be involved in the process which will hopefully prevent problems later on by identifying issues early. The client can even use the MVP to test it and identify bugs before they are ultimately fixed after release.

The client can use the MVP to test it and identify bugs before they are ultimately fixed after release.

How is the client involved in step two? By letting them see what you have created, you give them a chance to participate in the process of creating the product and even assist in testing it. This allows for a more effective collaboration between both of you. This can also give your client a greater level of confidence in the development process. By helping them test, you are also preventing bugs from cropping up which will save time and money in the long run.

In step three, we have created the product. This is a rough draft of what clients will ultimately receive and it needs to be refined. The main issue that you need to think about here is what problems have been identified during the process so far and how they are going to be solved now. When you have started out with a MVP, you will have identified the most basic steps that are needed to be taken. Your focus now has to change because the details will no longer be relevant.

It is important to remember that building a product and making it available for release is not the end of development. Once you realize this, it will make you more receptive to seeing problems or challenges as they arise and deal with them accordingly. This also makes your client more comfortable and gives them a greater level of confidence in your work.

Lean for AI Startups may not be suitable for every type of project. However, it is a valuable tool that can be used to create simple products without a huge amount of overheads. It can also help existing or new clients understand the process by which you operate and how they can be involved from the beginning. This means that you and your client will have a better understanding of exactly what is being done and where the priorities lie.

The Lean approach may not be suitable for every type of project. It has a lot of benefits when you need to accommodate changing requirements and changes in direction. The main advantage here is that it allows you to think about what you are doing and why, rather than simply reacting. It allows your client to learn more about the development process so they can become an active participant and lets you create the best possible product in the shortest amount of time possible. But this doesn't mean that it should be used for everything.

Sometimes, you need to create a more complex product without having the time to be constantly refining it. Or you might want to explain your development process in a way that makes sense for your chosen audience. It is also worth noting that Lean principles are aimed at reducing waste and making products as good as possible, or even perfect. This means that if you are creating an application which will have relatively set specifications, or has no need for changing requirements, the lean approach won't be useful.

So what's next? The lean approach is most useful when you are starting out. A lot of AI Startups don't have the resources to work on software projects, so they have to be as lean and efficient as possible. This means that they have no choice but to embrace the lean approach without losing their focus on quality.

Taking this approach into account is not easy and it can take time and effort to get your head around it, especially if you have never done it before. But the benefits are there to be taken advantage of. The lean approach allows you to create a product that not only works, but also works well. You can get to the finished product faster without losing sight of quality in the process.

8. DIFFERENT ROLE IN AI PRODUCT DESIGN AND DEVELOPMENT

Product design and development is a complex process that

involves many different skills. It would be impossible for one person to have all of the necessary skills, so it is essential that the role of product designer and developer be separated into two jobs.

A product designer's responsibility is to come up with an idea for a product. They then sketch out a prototype and put together a presentation of their ideas to a client or business partner. The duties of a product designer can also include designing the packaging of the product and the materials that will be used to make it. The product designer may also do some market research to find out what consumers would like to see in a new product.

A product developer, on the other hand, is responsible for working on different stages of production. They are in charge of making sure that the prototype is transformed into a finished product that is ready for public consumption. They may also handle the manufacturing process.

Many different companies have hired both product designers and product developers, but not necessarily at the same time. Having both roles in one person's job description would cause the designer to discover problems with the products during production, when they should have already been detected. As a result, a company may choose to hire one person to do everything and another person to do nothing at all.

There is an important difference between a designer and a developer. Product designers usually have experience in product design, while developers have experience in production. A designer is also a creative thinker and an inventor who can assemble all of their ideas into a final product.

Having two separate jobs for the same job title would benefit both the designer and the developer. The designer would be able to concentrate on making an idea come to life, which often is difficult because he or she will not be working with the developer during this process. The developer, on the other hand, would be able to use his or her experience in production to make corrections along the way.

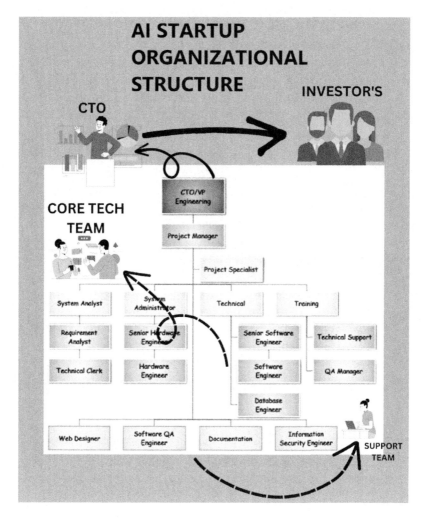

Fig 8. Typical AI Startup Organizational Structure

It is difficult to put a number on how many jobs this would create, but the general consensus is that it would create more jobs. If a company has two separate job titles for each role, they would have to hire four people. However, if both roles were combined into one job description, they could hire six people instead of four because the developer would have more experience in production than a designer.

Transforming the prototype into a finished product involves many

117

different tasks. A product developer has to make sure that all the parts of the product are made properly and there are no imperfections. They must also double check that the product is safe for consumers and that it meets all government regulations. They must also make sure that customers can easily use the item they have purchased.

Product developers also have to make sure that their product is cost efficient, so they need to work with engineers on new ways to manufacture a certain item at a lower cost. They will also be able to ensure that consumers will be able to use their products, so they must work with marketers on how the product should be promoted. Product developers don't just design a product; they also take part in shaping the way the product is marketed.

Product designers, on the other hand, have a lot less to do. They are creative thinkers who come up with new ideas and make those into real products. They also have to come up with new ideas for different types of products.

The two positions are very different. Product designers often will not interact with the product developer during the development process, but they may interact with the marketing department in order to make sure that their product will be marketed properly. The differences between product designers and developers is illustrated in this example:

"A Product Designer works on creating an idea for a new product and sketches various possibilities. A Product Developer then works on making that concept into a real product, including all of the production aspects."

Product design is the foundation of any company. Without new and improved products, a business would not be able to stay competitive. Product design is also simply fun to do. Anyone who likes working with their hands will find this position interesting.

Product development is a process that involves many different skills. If a company has a new idea for a product, one person does not have to do everything. Product developers and product designers have many different duties that they will both work on together. Together, they can transform an idea into an actual product that is ready to be sold to the public.

Product design first appeared in the early nineteenth century. Mass production of goods was becoming more and more popular and companies needed someone who could come up with new products for consumers.

8.1 CTO ROLE IN AI PRODUCT DESIGN AND DEVELOPMENT

Many companies and organizations define the role of a Chief

Technology Officer as one that is responsible for the company's technology, including research and development. A CTO can prepare a strategy for where technology should be used in their organization. Additionally, they may provide guidance on integrating new technologies with existing systems.

In a business setting, a chief technology officer works in an advisory capacity to the CEO and other senior executives in order to help them meet their objectives. The CTO is responsible for gathering information on market trends and potential opportunities. They can then present ideas to the executive staff on how those trends might best be addressed through emerging technologies.

CTO Main Responsibilities In AI Product Design and Development are:

1. Defining The Technology Strategy.

A CTO may have authority in determining the size of a company's development team and how it should be directed. A CTO presents an organization's technology vision to the CEO and other top executives through a strategy document that outlines how technology can help achieve the organization's business objectives.

2. Research And Development Initiatives.

Research and development initiatives may be a major part of the CTO's role. In some companies, the CTO is solely responsible for managing research and development functions. At other companies, a CTO is primarily responsible for guiding research strategy but also need to get involved in specific projects based on their strategic importance. In either case, the CTO has a major role in defining what type of products should be developed and ensuring that they are completed on time.

3. Technology Evaluation.

CTOs are responsible for evaluating emerging technologies and how they might be integrated within the company's current system.

Some companies also have a separate technology evaluation department that reviews emerging technologies for their business impact before the CTO takes action on them.

4. Interfacing With Third-Party Vendors.

Many companies use third-party vendors to assist with product development and integration. The CTO is in charge of the organization's interactions with the vendor.

5. Technology Training And Education.

Depending on the type of technology involved, some companies make it a priority to provide ongoing education and training to their employees related to it. Some companies have formal online courses that employees can participate in. Other companies may train their employees through educational programs such as seminars or conferences. In some companies, the CTO may also be responsible for developing software that provides information on how to use the new technology.

6. Developing Business Case For Technology.

CTOs often take a business approach to developing new technology. They use their knowledge of the business to evaluate potential products based on how it will enhance their operations and ultimately improve their bottom line. They can assist in presenting this information to senior management for review prior to beginning development activities with customers or third-party vendors.

7. Other Responsibilities.

CTOs may also have additional responsibilities for other functions within the organization, such as organizational development or human resources.

CTO has various tasks to perform and A CTO should develop these skills over the time:

In some companies, a separate chief information officer (CIO) is responsible for technology management and directing IT initiatives. Before a CIO was hired, the company's CTO might have done those tasks. But a CIO may be involved in fewer or more of the tasks throughout their career in IT.

8.1.1 CTO ROLE IN BUILDING MVP

In the AI startup development environment CTO actively

involved in the POC, Prototype, MVP and final product development.

Why We Need POC (Proof Of Concept)

In Agile development is all about making constant progress. That's why, in order to ensure that the product is heading in the right direction, it's important to have a POC (Proof of Concept). A POC helps to validate the idea behind the product and make sure that it can actually be implemented. It also allows the development team to experiment with different technologies and approaches to see what works best.

Having a POC is especially important when developing new features or products, as it reduces the risk of building something that might not actually be usable. A POC can also help to improve the chances of success for a product or feature by providing a proof of concept. This can be especially helpful when pitching the product to potential investors or partners. By having a POC, you can show that the product is viable and has a chance of being successful.

Finally, a POC can help to speed up development by allowing the team to focus on the most important aspects of the product. This can save a lot of time eventually, as it means that the team can spend more time on refining the product and less time on trying to figure out how to make it work. A POC helps to validate the idea behind the product and make sure that it can actually be implemented. It also allows the development team to experiment with different technologies and approaches to see what works best.

Fig 8.1 Steps In Creating The POC

Having a POC is especially important when developing new features or products, as it reduces the risk of building something that might not actually be usable. A POC can also be used to test out a new idea with potential customers. This can help to validate the idea and get feedback on what they would actually want from the product. It can also help to build hype for the product before it is actually released. How to Create a Proof of Concept There is no one-size-fits-all approach to creating a POC.

The best way to create one will depend on the specific product or feature being developed. However, there are some general steps that can be followed when creating a POC.

1. **Identify the Problem** - The first step is to identify the problem that the product or feature is trying to solve. This will help to define the scope of the POC and what needs to be accomplished.

2. **Research Potential Solutions** - Once the problem has been identified, research potential solutions. This can involve looking at similar products or features that have been

developed, as well as patents.

3. **Identify the Best Solution** - Once these solutions have been identified, it is then important to narrow them down to the best solution. This can be done by assessing various factors, such as cost, feasibility and technology.

4. **Develop a Proof of Concept** - The next stage is to develop a 'proof of concept', which is a demonstration that the proposed solution actually works. This can be done using a prototype or by carrying out a small-scale test.

5. **Analyze the Results** - Once the proof of concept has been developed, it is then important to analyze the results. This will help to determine whether the solution actually solves the problem in question and whether it is viable for further development.

Why We Need Minimum Viable Product (MVP)

The minimum viable product is a product with the minimum number of features needed to satisfy early customers, and to provide feedback for future product development. The idea behind the MVP is that a company can reduce the risk of developing a product that no one wants by releasing a bare-bones version of the product and then listening to customer feedback.

The company can then use that feedback to decide which features to add or remove from future versions of the product. The MVP approach has been popularized by startups, who often have limited resources and need to move quickly. However, the MVP approach can be used by any company that wants to reduce the risk of developing a product that no one wants.

Ten benefits of creating a minimum viable product

1. Helps you validate your idea quickly and cheaply
2. Reduces the risk of developing something your users may not even want
3. Helps you get feedback early on and iterate based on that feedback
4. Gives you a clear vision of what your final product should look like
5. helps you focus on the most important features first
6. Helps ensure that your team is aligned on the product's vision
7. Encourages faster development cycles
8. Makes it easier to raise funds based on a working prototype
9. Increases chances of success by reducing scope creep
10. Help build a culture of experimentation within your team

Steps In Creating Minimum Viable Product

Creating a minimum viable product, or MVP, is a process that every startup should go through. An MVP is the simplest version of your product that you can put in front of potential customers to get feedback.

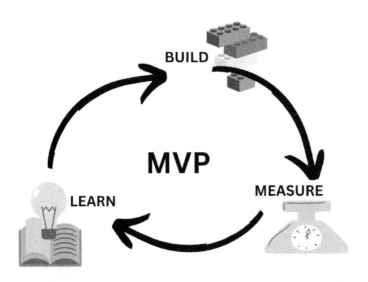

Fig 8.2 Steps In Creating MVP

The goal of an MVP is not to have a fully featured product, but rather to validate your assumptions about your product and your market.

Here are the steps you need to take to create an MVP:

1. Define your problem and your solution
2. Identify your target market and customer segments
3. Create a list of features for your MVP
4. Prioritize those features based on customer feedback
5. Build and launch your MVP
6. Test and measure the results
7. Iterate on your MVP based on feedback

Prototype Development

Prototypes are essential for product development. They help you validate your product idea, test assumptions, and gather feedback from users early in the process. Creating a prototype doesn't have to be complicated or time-consuming. In fact, the goal should be to create a basic prototype that you can use to test your ideas and get feedback from potential users as quickly as possible.

There are many ways to create prototypes, but one of the simplest and most effective methods is to use a tool like Balsamiq Mockups. With Balsamiq, you can create clickable wireframes that look and feel like real software applications.

This makes it easy to get feedback on the overall flow and design of your product before you start building it. Once you have a basic prototype that you're happy with, you can start adding more detailed designs and functionality. But even at this stage, it's important to remember that your goal should be to create a working product, not just a pretty one.

Don't get bogged down in details that don't matter right now; focus on creating something that solves the problem you set out to solve. To put it simply, this means adding user flows and design details in order of importance. "Essential" is different for every product, but in general, the primary user goal is the most important.

Next up is ensuring that you have a good foundation for future expansion. Only then should you begin to worry about things like branding, color schemes, and other details. Prototyping allows you to bring your product to life, test it with users, and iterate on your design. After you've developed a prototype, you can present it to investors/stakeholders to get buy-in and funding.

Final Thoughts Creating a product MVP is a careful balancing act. On the one hand, you want to create something that provides value to your users and solves their problems. On the other hand, you want to keep your costs low and your time to market short.

The key is to focus on providing value first and ensuring that the technology you use supports dramatic agile innovation. One of the best ways to dramatically increase your data delivery agility and reduce your costs is to implement a reactive data architecture.

By focusing on the following key principles, you can continuously and incrementally evolve your architecture to support your business objectives while reducing the rate at which your applications become obsolete.

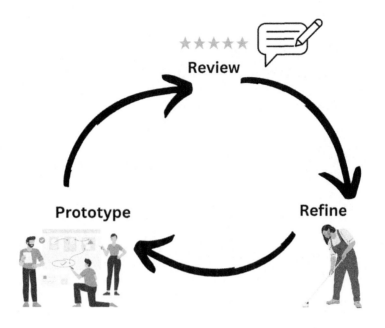

Fig 8.3 Steps In Building A Perfect Prototype For Your AI Products

Data Services Over Data Structure One of the key principles of reactive data architecture is to focus on data services over data structures. By focusing on data services over data structure, you can dramatically increase your agility while reducing your overall costs.

In a traditional data architecture, the data is stored in a static data structure. The data structure is then used by the application to access the data. This approach requires a significant amount of upfront planning and design to ensure that the data structure meets the needs of the application. In a reactive data architecture, the data is stored in a dynamic data service.

Steps In Creating Prototype

1. Define the problem you are trying to solve

2. Research your competitors and understand their solutions

3. Brainstorm and come up with multiple solutions to the

problem

4. Create a mockup or prototype of the best solution

5. Test the prototype with potential users and get feedback

6. Iterate on the design based on feedback received

7. Launch the final product

Five Benefits Of Creating Prototype

1. Prototypes help simplify complex designs, making them easier to understand.

2. Prototypes can be used to test various aspects of the design, such as functionality, usability, and maneuverability.

3. Prototypes can help identify potential problems with a design before it goes into production.

4. Prototypes allow designers to experiment with different ideas and solutions.

5. Prototypes can be used to generate feedback from users and stakeholders.

8.2 SOFTWARE ARCHITECT ROLE IN AI PRODUCT DESIGN AND DEVELOPMENT

As a Software Architect, you play an important role in the design and development of AI products. You are responsible for analyzing feature requirements and leading the core development team. You must design, architect and implement solutions that meet business needs and serve as a trusted advisor to executive management.

Your ability to research, invent, design, build and maintain novel AI solutions is essential for success. You need to be up-to-date on the latest trends in AI technology and software development, staying informed of new technologies through conferences such as the Leading Edge Software Development Conference. Additionally, you should be comfortable working with AI hardware and software such as Python, Alternatives and other similar technologies.

You will also be responsible for product development, channeling customer feedback into useful insights that can help improve the product design process. To succeed in this role you must have excellent problem solving skills and be able to work independently or in teams when needed.

Software Architect Key Skills Are:

- Mathematical / Algorithmic Skills
- AI/ML knowledge
- Communication Skills
- Decision Making Skills
- Collaboration Skills

Software Architect role definition is: Software architects are the technical leaders of the software development team. They lead the team by providing guidance on architectural decisions and working with other team members to provide a vision for their product or solution. They represent their organization's needs and coordinate activities with other teams to meet these needs. They play a key role in the development of their organization's products, supporting the business needs and achieving project objectives.

Software Architect must know programming language, across many languages, in order to understand how technology works, then be able to tell programmers how the product should work. They are the bridge between people who build a product and people who use it.

They have a good understanding of how a product will be used. They set up guidelines for the team and design processes that help make requirements clear, leads to an efficient planning process, as well as easy communication between team members and developers.

8.3 UI/UX ROLE IN AI PRODUCT DESIGN AND DEVELOPMENT

Do you know what role the User Interface and User Experience Designer plays in a company? Do you know how they think, what they do, and who their responsibilities are? If not, it's time that you learn more about this position to make sure your job is the right fit for yourself.

UI/UX usability are important in the AI product development process because they help to ensure that products are easy to use and understand. There are a number of different methods that can be used to assess UI UX usability, including: - Questionnaires - Interviews - Focus groups - Heuristic evaluations - User testing - Cognitive walkthroughs.

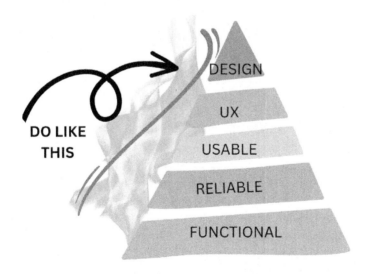

Fig 8.4 How To Create Outstanding Design For AI Product.

How Usability impact on Product Development?

In product development, usability has a significant impact on how successful a product will be. If a product is difficult to use, customers will be less likely to use it and may even return it. A product that is easy to use, on the other hand, will be more likely to be used and may even be recommended to others. In the context of software development, usability is often referred to as user experience (UX). Designers and developers must take UX into consideration when creating a new product, as a poor UX can lead to poor customer satisfaction and even sales.

What is beauty? Beauty is a quality that is appreciated for its aesthetic value. It is often associated with properties such as harmony, symmetry, and balance. Beauty is often said to be in the eye of the beholder, as what one person finds beautiful may not be seen as such by someone else.

The role of the UI/UX Designer has evolved over the last few years, but typically they are tasked with making products easier to use and understand for both existing users and potential new users. It is very important that this person is a team player who works extremely well with the Product Manager or Product Owner and can determine which features need to be built next.

Building an AI product requires careful UI/UX design. As a designer, tasked with the challenge of creating a product that is both user-friendly and efficient. Designer must take into consideration how to create an interface that users trust and understand. This means considering how to make the UX localized, as well as taking into account user expectations, experiences, and levels of trust in AI.

To ensure success, it's important to keep in mind seven basic AI UX principles: usability, scalability, efficiency, learnability, adaptability, security and privacy. Usability involves making sure the user interface is easy to use; scalability involves making sure the software can be used across different platforms; efficiency ensures the system works quickly and accurately; learnability involves making sure users can quickly learn how to use the system; adaptability ensures that changes in technology don't require large modifications; security involves ensuring data remains private; and privacy ensures users' data remains confidential.

Designers must also be mindful when designing for AI products by taking into consideration contextual needs such as language or cultural differences. Additionally, using AI-based translation can help ensure design is localized for different cultures or languages. Ultimately, designers should keep in mind that not

This entry will give you an overview of what a User Interface (UI) Designer does.

What Is The Role Of A User Interface Designer?

The User Interface Designer (UI) is responsible for the look and feel of the website or application, including, but not limited to:

They make sure that each user can understand and use the platform in a way that makes sense to them. They deal with what you see on your screen, how one part of the system relates to another, and ensuring that the entire product clearly communicates what it's supposed to do. The user interface designer's goal is to make sure you don't have to think about how to use the application. It should be intuitive and obvious.

They make sure that each user can understand and use the platform in a way that makes sense to them. They deal with what you see on your screen, how one part of the system relates to another, and ensuring that the entire product clearly communicates what it's supposed to do. The user interface designer's goal is to make sure you don't have to think about how to use the application. It should be intuitive and obvious.

What Does A UI Designer Do?

The first thing that a user interface designer does is of course, research. They will go through every aspect of the product and look at what we currently have in place for our design, so that they understand exactly how existing users are using it, and how hard it is for them to get things done without any trouble. This research also includes user personas and market research to get a better idea of who our users are and what they expect from the product. They then use this research to develop the most effective way to design the new user interface, taking all of these things into consideration.

They will go through every aspect of the product and look at what we currently have in place for our design, so that they understand exactly how existing users are using it, and how hard it is for them to get things done without any trouble.

This research also includes user personas and market research to get a better idea of who our users are and what they expect from the product. They then use this research to develop the most effective way to design the new user interface, taking all of these things into consideration.

This involves creating user flow diagrams, wireframes and prototypes that will help flesh out the design, but we'll get into those in a minute.

What Does A UX Creature Do?

A User Experience Designer also goes through the same process of research and design, but they are also more concerned with how the user feels about using the product. They will use this research to develop personas, but will also look at emotional factors that go into designing a great user experience. They make sure that every aspect of your product is easy to understand and is intuitive so that users have no trouble completing tasks or navigating your product.

A User Experience Designer also goes through the same process of research and design, but they are also more concerned with how the user feels about using the product. They will use this research to develop personas, but will also look at emotional factors that go into designing a great user experience. They make sure that every aspect of your product is easy to understand and is intuitive so that users have no trouble completing tasks or navigating your product.

They will take your research and create detailed scenarios to show

how real users are likely to interact with the product, before moving on to the design and development process. They are also responsible for usability testing and making sure that your product is intuitive enough for your users.

They will take your research and create detailed scenarios to show how real users are likely to interact with the product, before moving on to the design and development process. They are also responsible for usability testing and making sure that your product is intuitive enough for your users.

How Minimal UI/UX Is Key To Success Of AI Product?

Minimal UI/UX is key to the success of any AI product. With the growth of industries such as e-commerce and web development, UI/UX design has become essential. AI products rely on data collected from analytics, user base, product catalogues, and other sources to make decisions.

UX/UI design is a multidisciplinary process that involves five main phases: setting KPIs to measure expectations, creating a user interface with empathy for the users, adding features and improving workflow, solving usability issues to create a pleasant online experience, and ensuring that the application caters to user needs.

By carefully designing the UX/UI of an AI product, developers are able to create successful products that provide users with an intuitive and enjoyable experience. Minimal UI/UX design allows for simpler applications that are easy to use and understand—making it key for the success of any AI product.

8.4 SOFTWARE DEVELOPER ROLE IN AI PRODUCT
DESIGN AND DEVELOPMENT

Software developers play an important role in AI product design and development.

Software developers need a variety of skills to build Artificial Intelligence (AI) products. These include mathematics, algebra, calculus, statistics, big data, data mining, data science, machine learning, cognitive computing, text analytics, natural language processing, R programming language, Hadoop framework and Spark platform. Knowing the fundamentals of these fields is essential for any AI developer to make a meaningful contribution.

Furthermore, Software developers who wish to work in the field of Artificial Intelligence (AI) must possess certain skills and knowledge of AI libraries. Programming languages such as Python, Java and Scala are essential for developers to become proficient in AI. Knowledge of popular AI libraries such as TensorFlow, Café, and Torch is also necessary.

Additionally, software developers need to have a good understanding of math, algebra, calculus, statistics and big data. With the help of AI libraries and algorithms, developers are able to create features for AI programs and software.

Python is the language of choice for most AI developers due to its readability and availability of pre-designed libraries that optimize the development process. By leveraging the right data from various sources and properly utilizing the available resources, software developers are able to bridge the skill gap and develop robust AI applications.

Finally, AI developers should be able to use algorithms to automate processes and make programmers more productive. This requires knowledge of how algorithms work and how they can be used to streamline processes and reduce waste. With this knowledge in hand any AI developer can create innovative solutions that will transform the way the world works today.

Software developers can use also AI and machine learning based tools, software developers can make the product design process more accurate and efficient. Some of the benefits of using AI tools for product design and development include:

1. Increased accuracy: AI tools can help software developers create more accurate designs, as they can take into account a wider range of factors and variables.

2. Increased efficiency: AI tools can automate some of the design and development processes, making them more efficient.

3. Better user experience: AI tools can help create better user experiences by creating more personalized and customized products.

For example, AIDA (Artificial Intelligence Design Assistant) is a tool that can be used to help with product design. Senior software engineers specializing in defense and intelligence applications may also be involved in AI product design and development, in addition to product designers who work with C3 AI Studio. Finally, sales development roles are also related to this area of the industry. All these professionals contribute to making sure that AI products are designed effectively and meet customer expectations.

9. AI STARTUPS CHALLENGES

If you're thinking about starting a software development startup, be prepared to face some complications. If so, this chapter is for you! We'll explore the challenges faced by AI Startups. After all, this is the new frontier of technology today where more and more emerging companies are trying to compete for customers.

AI startups face numerous challenges in order to succeed. The most common ones include fundraising, marketing, data and lack of customization for each and every AI project. Fundraising is an area that startups need to become well-versed in, as they often require additional investment from venture capitalists. Marketing is also a key challenge for AI startups as they need to create a buzz around their products and services by getting the right message across to their consumers.

Data sets are also important for AI startups, as they need to determine the right data set for their projects in order to reap the most benefits from the technology. Additionally, there can be a lack of customization for each and every AI project which requires creative solutions from the startup team itself.

Another challenge that AI startups face is a lack of business ailment. Companies may not fully understand or appreciate the value of integrating artificial intelligence into their operations or products which can cause delays in development or implementation. Furthermore, there may be concerns over trustworthiness

WHAT CHALLENGES I FACED WITH MY AI STARTUPS CHALLENGES

Startups leveraging Artificial Intelligence (AI) technology have seen tremendous growth in the past five years. While AI offers immense potential to startups, there are also significant challenges associated with its adoption. The top five challenges that need to be addressed by startups include determining the right data set, data quality and privacy, overcoming trust deficit, managing limited knowledge, and achieving human-level performance.

Determining the right data set is essential for AI to work accurately and effectively. To ensure this, startups must have access to large amount of high-quality data sets that can be used for training and testing purposes. Additionally, due to the sensitive nature of such data, startups must also have protocols in place for securely collecting and storing it.

The trust deficit associated with AI remains another challenge for startups as it is often seen as an untrustworthy technology by consumers. This can be overcome by providing transparency into how AI works and through increasing user engagement with products or services powered by AI.

WHAT RISK I FACED WITH MY AI STARTUP

AI startups face a number of risks that can derail their success. These five main risks are lack of AI implementation traceability, inadequate data, low customer desirability and commercial viability, uneven success rates of AI deployments, and global competition.

Lack of AI implementation traceability can lead to public backlash and criticism when the results of AI-powered products are unclear or misunderstood. Companies need to be able to easily track the implementation process for their projects in order to avoid this risk.

Inadequate data is another major risk for AI startups. Data needs to be consistent, up-to-date, and of high quality in order to support successful AI implementations. Companies should take the time to assess the quality of their data before they proceed with any projects.

Customer desirability and commercial viability are two other factors that companies need to consider when assessing risks associated with their AI investments. They need to determine whether the problem they are trying to solve is even worth solving in the first place.

WHAT PROBLEMS I FACED WITH MY AI STARTUP

If your team has any experience in software development, the list of problems may seem daunting. Some of these issues include:

- Finding good employees with relevant skillsets can be difficult due to high competition for their services in various areas of tech and possible wage pressures from tech giants like Google and Microsoft.

- The cost of software development, especially when you're just starting out, can be extremely expensive. This is because you will need to hire programmers and other tech-related experts to help build your product.

- You may also need to invest on top of the employees who are needed to develop the product. This means some of your team might become employees rather than self-employed workers if the start-up fails.

- The cost of renting office space in Silicon Valley can be high, which may eat up a lot of the money saved from operating at a lower cost and with fewer employees.

- There are also other costs involved aside from the developers' salaries such as accounting, legal services, etc.

- Hiring freelancers also adds up to the financial burden of your business.

- Finding good network to solve marketing issues is also crucial since this is what leads to more customers for your business.

- In most cases, you won't be able to pick the customers to serve since they will be picked by your network.

- If you're planning to sell your product, then you must make sure that it's not just a commodity. You must also make sure that it benefits the customers and other users.

- Staying up to date with technology trends is also important if you want to stay competitive against other software development start-ups.

- You need to also make sure that your team has a good knowledge of marketing and development so you can properly build and market your product.

- The management style might have to change if you will have employees rather than self-employed workers. For instance, managing tasks that involve teamwork may need more
communication channels since they are a group effort--not solely leadership's responsibility.

- While the risks of starting a software development startup can be stacked against you, the return on investments can be more rewarding than one would expect.

9.1 DATA DISTRACTION IN AI PRODUCT DEVELOPMENT

AI needs data to accurately estimate flu activity. For example, researchers have developed an AI tool that uses real-world state and regional data from the US and Japan to make forecasts. Additionally, Google Trends data can also be used to improve the accuracy of flu estimates. Furthermore, location data can provide robust longer-term insights on flu activity. However, it is important to note that this data should be diverse in order to produce accurate results.

AI models and machine learning algorithms need to be trained with different data sets. Training data is labeled data used to teach AI models or machine learning algorithms to make proper decisions. This data can come from various sources such as the internet, existing databases, or created synthetically. Factors like geography, market demographics, and competition within your niche hinder the availability of relevant datasets. It's the most crucial aspect that makes algorithm training possible and explains why machine learning became so popular in recent years.

It is true that there can be a fear of having too little data when developing an AI product. The key to overcoming this is to focus on 'creatively adequate' AI solutions, as these do not require large datasets and can still be effective.

Additionally, it is important to understand the concept of DataOps which combines software development and manufacturing operations to make sense of data coming in from devices. Cross-skilling and growing T-shaped team members is also important as this allows teams to become more knowledgeable in different areas which can help them think more creatively. Finally, having a mission statement which affects day-to-day behavior in the workplace can help employees understand the goals of the project and act accordingly.

HOW TO OVERCOME DATA DISTRACTION

Organizations(team) should focus on using AI to solve specific problems and ensure that data is used effectively. This can be done by setting clear objectives, understanding the data available, and investing in user education. It is also important to ensure that AI products are subject to product liability laws, as well as have users have power over their data. Additionally, it is important to use machine learning and analytics to identify data that is seldom or never used and recommend that it be thrown away. Finally, organizations should invest in robust testing and prototyping processes to ensure that AI products are reliable and effective.

9.2 HOW TO AVOID SOFTWARE DEVELOPMENT AI STARTUPS FAILURES

Developers in a software development startup may experience failure in different ways. For any company seeking to build a product in the market, here are some of the most common reasons for failure.

LACK OF PROPER FUNDING

Many companies lack the necessary funding to see the product through all the necessary phases of growth and launch. Venture capitalists often have limited funds and can't invest them all in businesses they believe will succeed.

How to get funding AI startups

Getting funding for an AI startup can be a daunting task, but it doesn't have to be. With the right strategy and a well-crafted pitch deck, it is possible to secure the necessary funds to get your business off the ground. To increase your chances of success, AI startups should focus on doing research and development testing with real customers and creating a strong marketing and sales approach. Additionally, it may also be beneficial to explore investment opportunities from angel investors, incubators, venture capitalists or even Google Brain founder Andrew Ng's AI Fund. By following these tips, entrepreneurs can create an effective plan for getting the funding they need for their AI startups.

LACK OF EXPERIENCE

A developer with no past experience may be unable to bring new ideas and technology to market. He or she lacks the necessary skills and knowledge needed to create a viable product. The startup may fail because of a lack of innovation, which is impossible to find in an inexperienced developer.

How to Achieve product-market fit

Achieving product-market fit with AI technologies requires careful consideration and strategic planning. First, it is important to identify the core function, audience, and desired use of the AI product. Then evaluate the data pipelines to ensure they are properly configured for inputting and outputting the necessary data. Once the product design is set in place, it is essential to differentiate your product from competitors in order to stand out in the market.

Content creators and influencers can help market your product by showcasing its features, while product recommendations can provide a more personalized experience for customers. Lastly, conducting market research and gathering customer data will enable you to create an AI-based solution tailored to fit their needs. With these steps in place, businesses will be well on their way to achieving a successful product-market fit with their AI technologies.

LACK OF MANAGEMENT

Management services are also important for any startup that seeks to build a product in the market. Managers are the ones who keep the company running smoothly and make sure products are finished on time. Without them, a startup may fail.

How to scope the AI product knowledge managers

As organizations strive to stay ahead of the competition, they are increasingly turning to AI product knowledge managers. An AI product knowledge manager is responsible for the development and maintenance of an organization's AI-based knowledge management system. This involves creating no-code DIY platforms that allow customers to easily find relevant solutions with AI-backed capabilities.

Typically, an AI product knowledge manager will have a strong understanding of artificial intelligence and machine learning, as well as domain expertise in these disciplines. They must be able to coordinate different team members in order to collect and manage data, build prototypes for new products using AI, create and maintain a knowledge base, and develop strategies for customer engagement. Additionally, they need to ensure that customer feedback is incorporated into the system in order to continually improve customer experience.

AI product knowledge managers are also expected to stay up-to-date with emerging technologies in order to provide their organization with the best possible solutions.

LACK OF AI SKILLED DEVELOPERS

Finding AI programmers is also a difficult task for any startup that seeks to build a product in the market. Manpower is limited and companies need to use experienced people who understand the technologies they use. However, some companies cannot find experienced people, so they have no choice but to hire unqualified developers who don't know how to build products with their technologies.

How to Hire and trai AI software developers

Hiring and training AI software developers is an important part of any organization's success. With the right team of professionals, businesses can leverage the power of Artificial Intelligence (AI) to create innovative solutions and improve their operations. To ensure that they have the best talent available, organizations should look for experienced AI software developers who have a strong understanding of programming languages, algorithms, and data structures.

Additionally, they should also consider investing in training programs to help their developers stay up-to-date with the latest technologies and trends in AI development. By doing so, businesses can ensure that their teams are well-equipped to handle any challenges that may arise during the development process.

LACK OF MARKETING KNOWLEDGE

Selling the digital product is challenging if there is no knowledge of the marketing principles and techniques, especially for AI Startups. Companies that don't have these things in place also tend to fail. Marketing is a very important aspect that no startup can ignore.

AI Startups Marketing Strategy

AI startups are revolutionizing the way marketers reach their customers. By leveraging AI technology, these startups are able to segment customers, personalize campaigns, and optimize messaging for maximum impact. AI-powered marketing enables marketers to make data-driven decisions and create a more personalized brand expression.

This technology is especially useful in digital marketing where speed is essential. AI tools use customer data and profiles to learn how to best communicate with customers in order to drive conversions. 6sense, Bluecore, and Near are just a few of the top 10 startups developing AI for marketing. With the help of these companies, marketers can take their strategies to the next level and reach their target audiences more effectively than ever before.

LACK OF MONEY

Of course, any product will not succeed as long as there is no money to back it. The lack of funding may be due to a lack of venture capital, which occurs when the company doesn't have enough investors and investors are tired of investing in AI Startups.

How to keep cash flow

Starting an AI startup can be a daunting task, but with the right strategies, you can ensure that your business has the cash flow it needs to succeed. To keep money flowing into your AI startup, consider utilizing crowdfunding platforms like Kickstarter and Indiegogo to raise capital.

Additionally, take advantage of the latest technological advancements such as artificial intelligence (AI) to predict and manage cash flow. Modeling various scenarios will help you understand the extent of your current cash runway and plan for the timing and amount of funds needed. Finally, make sure to keep your invoices neat and clean by including important details, payment preferences, terms (with links if possible), and other necessary information. By following these steps, you can ensure that your AI startup has a steady stream of cash flow.

9.3 EU/US LAWS ON AI AND PRIVACY CONCERNS

Many countries around the world have taken legal and regulatory actions for Artificial Intelligence (AI) across nine different areas. 193 countries have adopted the first-ever global agreement on the Ethics of Artificial Intelligence, which is endorsed by all 29 Member states of the UN Educational, Scientific and Cultural Organisation (UNESCO).

In Brazil, lawmakers have passed a bill that outlines legal regulations for AI. Austria is also making efforts to integrate AI into judicial policies. In Europe, Belgium, Estonia, Germany, Finland, Hungary and other countries have laws in place that allow for the testing of AI-driven technologies.

Overall, countries are taking steps to ensure that AI is regulated in a responsible manner. This includes setting standards for privacy and data protection, as well as considering ethical implications of AI applications.

EU LAW ON AI

The European Union's AI Act is a proposed law on artificial intelligence (AI) – the first law on AI by a major regulator anywhere. It sets out horizontal rules for the development, commodification and use of AI-driven products, services and systems within the EU.

The regulation divides AI systems into three categories: unacceptable-risk AI systems, high-risk AI systems, and other AI systems. It creates a process for self-certification and government oversight of many categories of high-risk AI systems, and imposes tailored obligations on actors at different parts of the value chain, from "providers" of AI systems to "users". The aim is to ensure that

AI is human-centric and trustworthy while making the EU a world-class hub for AI.

USA LAW ON AI

Despite AI's ubiquity across every technology and healthcare field, there is no comprehensive federal legislation on AI in the United States. The National AI Initiative, which became law in 2021, has the mission to coordinate a program across the entire US federal government to accelerate the development and adoption of AI. Last week, the US White House Office of Science and Technology Policy (OSTP) released a "Blueprint for an AI Bill of Rights" along with five core principles that would govern the use of AI including creating safe and effective systems, discrimination prevention, privacy protection, transparency and accountability.

The FTC has not promulgated AI-specific regulations but issued a memo in April 2021 to make and deploy artificial intelligence more responsibly and limit AI-based surveillance. Companies can avoid potential legal issues by understanding state privacy laws that will affect AI.

Privacy Concerns With The Advancement Of Artificial Intelligence

As Artificial Intelligence (AI) continues to become more integrated into our lives and economy, it brings with it a number of privacy concerns. AI's ability to collect and analyze massive amounts of data on individuals without their knowledge or consent can be used for malicious purposes. With the advancement of AI in the year 2030, it is important to consider how to ensure that individuals' privacy is protected from potential abuses.

The use of AI-powered technologies such as big data and other EDTs presents both risks and opportunities for both businesses and consumers. Companies can use this data to accurately target their services or products at specific consumer groups. However, there are also risks associated with the misuse of this data, including the potential for discrimination or misusing personal information for marketing purposes.

At the same time, advances in AI have enabled powerful tools such as facial recognition technology that has been used by governments around the world for surveillance purposes. This technology can be used to monitor citizens without their consent or knowledge and can be used to target certain groups of people based on race, gender or religion.

In order to address these privacy concerns, governments must create regulations that protect individuals' rights while allowing companies to continue innovating with AI-driven technologies.

For example, laws should be put in place that require companies to gain explicit consent from users before collecting any personal information and limit how long they can hold onto this data. Additionally, measures should be taken to ensure that any facial recognition technology is used in a way that safeguards against discrimination and other privacy violations. The EU should also ensure that individuals have a right to know when facial recognition technology is being used and to have a say in how it is deployed. Regardless of the outcome of the EU's deliberations, facial recognition technology is likely to become a regular part of our lives.

10. AI IN THE YEAR 2030

It's hard to predict what the future holds, but one thing is for sure: Artificial Intelligence (AI) will play a major role in our lives by the year 2030. From self-driving cars to facial recognition technology and more, AI is changing the way we live and work. In this chapter, we'll explore how AI will shape our future world in the next decade.

AI in the year 2030 will be drastically different than today. By then, AI will no longer just be getting adopted with simple scenarios and applications, but instead be expected to detect life-threatening situations and have a major impact on life and society in urban cities. AI could even contribute up to $15.7 trillion to the global economy in 2030 - more than the current output of China and India combined! It is estimated that most AI will be used for marketing purposes by then, bombarding people with personalized ads and messages. In order to embrace an intelligent world through digital and intelligent systems, the One Hundred Year Study on Artificial Intelligence was launched in 2014. This long-term investigation focuses on understanding how AI will shape our lives in the future.

10.1 AI STARTUP IN YEAR 2030 FOR SMART CITIES, DIGITAL CURRENCY, ELECTRIC CARS, IOT AND QUANTUM COMPUTING

AI technology has advanced significantly in the decade since 2020, leading to the development of sophisticated AI startups that are transforming smart cities, digital currency, electric cars, IoT and quantum computing. These startups are leveraging the latest technologies such as artificial intelligence (AI), machine learning (ML), natural language processing (NLP), computer vision (CV) and blockchain to develop innovative solutions that have the potential to revolutionize these industries.

In smart cities, AI startups are using computer vision and predictive analytics to monitor traffic flows and detect anomalies. This data can then be used to optimize traffic signals or suggest alternative routes for drivers. Additionally, AI can be used for facial recognition for security purposes or for automated customer service in retail stores.

In digital currency, AI startups are leveraging blockchain technology and predictive analytics to create secure transactions and trading platforms. They are also using AI-driven bots for automated trading on cryptocurrency exchanges. Additionally, they are developing algorithms that analyze market data in real-time in order to identify patterns and predict price movements of cryptocurrencies.

For electric cars, AI startups are developing autonomous driving technologies that allow cars to drive themselves with minimal human intervention. This includes utilizing sensors, GPS

navigation systems and machine learning algorithms that enable vehicles to "think" on their own. Furthermore, these startups have begun exploring how artificial intelligence can be used to improve vehicle safety by detecting potential hazards ahead of time and taking corrective action if required.

In IoT applications, AI startups are exploring how they can enable vehicles to communicate with other vehicles and infrastructure (e.g., traffic lights and road signs) in order to avoid accidents and improve traffic flow. Overall, AI-powered startups are reimagining how vehicles are built, powered, and

operated in order to make them more efficient, sustainable, and safe.This report provides an overview of the AI in automotive landscape and includes profiles of 50+ startups that are developing AI-powered solutions for the automotive industry. The report also includes an overview of the major AI in automotive use cases, detailed analysis of AI in automotive startup ecosystem, and an overview of the major AI in automotive startups.

This report has been prepared by our team of analysts and experts, who have years of experience in the field of automotive technology and market analysis. The report provides an in-depth analysis of the AI in automotive landscape and includes detailed profiles of 50+ startups that are developing AI-powered solutions for the automotive industry. The report also includes an overview of the leading AI in automotive companies that are deploying AI technologies in their product and services.

10.2 WHAT CHALLENGES WILL FACE IN 2030 DUE TO AI

AI in the year 2030 is expected to be a major part of many industries and our daily lives, but it is not without its challenges. In 2030, AI will face numerous challenges, including creating safe and reliable hardware for autonomous cars and health care robots; addressing ethical issues such as privacy, fairness, and transparency; and understanding the implications of AI on the environment, communities, and an organization's bottom line.

Furthermore, it will be important to ensure that AI technologies are implemented in a timely manner with minimal lag time. As AI continues to grow exponentially in terms of data generated from edge computing and deep learning algorithms, it will be essential to find ways to handle both the sheer volume of data as well as the complexity of its use. Finally, with ever-evolving artificial intelligence technologies being adopted by enterprises worldwide, it is important to consider how people are going to interact with these systems as they become more prevalent in everyday life.

THE IMPACT OF AI ON EDUCATION

The impact of AI on education in 2030 is expected to be significant, with an estimated market size of over USD 80 billion. AI technology has the potential to revolutionize the way that people learn, enabling more personalized and efficient learning experiences. By 2030, AI is likely to be integrated into many aspects of education, including curriculum design, assessment and feedback systems, teaching materials and resources, and even student support services. AI can also help create new opportunities for collaboration and engagement between learners and their peers or instructors. Furthermore, AI can help drive cost savings for educational institutions by streamlining processes such as data management, forecasting and analytics.

With AI in place in most institutions by 2030, educators will need to equip themselves with the necessary knowledge and skills to take advantage of this technology. It is therefore essential that teachers receive adequate training on how to use these tools effectively in order to ensure that students are getting the highest quality education possible.

THE IMPACT OF AI ON BUSINESSES

The year 2030 is set to be an exciting one for AI and its related technologies. By then, it is estimated that around 70 percent of companies will have adopted at least one type of AI technology. This adoption could contribute up to $15.7 trillion to the global economy in 2030 – more than the current output of China and India combined.

AI can give businesses a competitive edge by providing tailored solutions for their specific problems. This close fit of solutions allows companies to save time and money, making them more efficient and cost-effective. Additionally, AI can help increase efficiency in the workplace by automating some processes such as customer service, data analytics, and fraud detection that would normally require manual labor.

The potential economic benefits from AI are immense – taking into account competition effects and transition costs it could potentially deliver additional economic output of about 1.2 percent a year over the next decade or so. This is why businesses should take advantage of this technology now in order to maximize their potential profits in the future.

Overall, as we move closer to 2030, AI will become increasingly important for businesses large and small as it provides access to tailor-made solutions that can help maximize profits while minimizing operational costs. It's a win-win situation for all involved!

THE IMPACT OF AI ON HEALTHCARE

The impact of Artificial Intelligence (AI) on healthcare in 2030 is expected to be profound. AI-powered predictive healthcare networks are predicted to reduce wait times, improve staff workflows and take on the ever-growing global healthcare needs. AI can help improve the experience of healthcare practitioners, global economy could create 40 million new health-sector jobs by 2030. The global artificial intelligence in healthcare market size is forecasted to reach USD 208.2 billion by 2030, increasing at a compound annual growth rate (CAGR) of 38.1%. It is also expected that AI will allow for earlier detection and diagnosis of some of our leading causes of disease, and we'll see greater use of at-home health technology such as virtual doctor visits and digital health records.

These advances will enable patients to receive better care with improved accuracy, accessibility, and cost savings. As a result, the quality of care delivered by healthcare professionals can be improved significantly.

THE IMPACT OF AI ON TRANSPORTATION

AI is expected to have a major impact on the transportation sector in 2030. According to Precedence Research, the global artificial intelligence (AI) in transportation market size is projected to surpass around USD 14.79 billion by 2030. There are many ways in which AI can improve transport services and revolutionize the industry, ranging from improving planning and organizing fleets to tracking containers, processing payments, and charging for services. AI could also potentially disrupt sectors such as healthcare, public safety, jobs, and even the environment if strategic cooperation between the public and private sectors is not taken into account.

AI advances are likely to add $13 trillion to global economic output by 2030, with road safety features being increasingly adopted by governments around the world. Technologies such as automated driving systems can help reduce traffic accidents and fatalities significantly. AI-based systems will also help speed up traffic flow and optimize routes for travelers more efficiently over time.

As AI technology continues to evolve in coming years, it will be important for governments worldwide to take steps that ensure its development is socially responsible. This includes developing regulations that protect citizens' data privacy while enabling them access to the benefits of smarter transport solutions enabled by AI technologies such as autonomous vehicles or smart cities infrastructure initiatives.

The Impacts of Artificial Intelligence on Employment and the Economy in 2030.

AI has the potential to revolutionize the global economy and create significant opportunities for job growth and economic prosperity. In 2030, AI is set to contribute up to $15.7 trillion to the global economy, more than the current output of China and India combined. This would represent a 26% increase in global GDP, compared to today's levels.

However, there are potential downsides as well; AI could lead to job losses in certain sectors, particularly lower-skilled jobs that are easier for robots or AI systems to do. It could also widen gaps between countries, companies and workers due to different access levels of technology.

In order for AI to benefit society at large, it is important that policy makers design strategies that promote responsible use of the technology while simultaneously creating an environment where people can access retraining programs or alternative job opportunities. Additionally, governments should focus on creating policies that ensure equitable access to AI technologies so that all countries can reap their full benefits.

THE ETHICAL IMPLICATIONS OF ARTIFICIAL INTELLIGENCE

The ethical implications of Artificial Intelligence (AI) are numerous and far-reaching. AI has the potential to revolutionize many aspects of our lives, from healthcare to transportation. However, with this potential comes the need for careful consideration of ethical issues, such as privacy, bias, and discrimination. In 2030, AI will be more ubiquitous than ever before and it is essential that the ethical considerations are addressed from the outset.

One issue that has been consistently raised in relation to AI is privacy. AI systems rely on large amounts of data for their operation and this data can be vulnerable to misuse or exploitation if not secured properly. It is therefore important that companies and governments ensure that they have robust systems in place to protect personal data collected through AI systems. Additionally, it is important that individuals understand what data they are sharing with companies when using their services and have appropriate control over how it is used.

Another key ethical issue surrounding AI relates to bias and discrimination. As AI is based on algorithms created by humans, there is a risk that certain biases may be embedded within them which could lead to unfair outcomes for certain individuals or groups of people. To address this risk, companies should strive for fairness in their implementation of AI systems by actively seeking out any potential biases present in their algorithms and introducing measures to mitigate them where possible.

By 2030, Artificial Intelligence will likely become an integral part of our daily lives and it is essential that we take the necessary steps now to ensure its use remains ethical , responsible and inclusive. intersection between human and machine learning

10.3 HOW TO PREPARE FOR THE FUTURE WITH AI IN MIND

The year 2030 is rapidly approaching and it is important to be prepared with Artificial Intelligence (AI) in mind. With AI expected to have a major influence on the way of life, there are several steps that can be taken now to ensure that individuals, organizations, and businesses are ready for the future.

First, individuals should make sure they have a basic understanding of AI and its potential implications. Understanding how AI works and what it can do will help prepare individuals for the changes it will bring in the near future. Additionally, those interested in using AI should consider taking courses or seminars on the subject to gain a deeper knowledge of how to utilize it effectively.

Organizations and businesses should also take steps to ensure they are able to use AI effectively by investing in research and development that focuses on incorporating it into their operations or services. Some companies may even want to focus on creating their own AI-based products or services as well as exploring partnerships with others who specialize in this field.

Finally, governments should consider making investments in digital infrastructure such as increased access to high-speed internet connections as well as providing resources for education on AI so more people have access to this technology. Governments may also want to explore policies that support the use of AI while protecting citizens from any unethical uses of these tools.

By taking these steps now, individuals, businesses, and governments can be better prepared for the future with Artificial

Intelligence in mind. The potential applications of this technology are limitless, and the benefits of harnessing its power will have a profound impact on consumer and business markets alike.

10.4 BENEFITS CAN WE EXPECT FROM ARTIFICIAL INTELLIGENCE BY 2030

By 2030, Artificial Intelligence (AI) is expected to have a major impact on our lives. AI has the potential to revolutionize how we do everyday tasks and provide us with unprecedented opportunities. We can expect AI to make jobs easier, increase productivity, and improve access to services.

AI can help us automate mundane tasks and make them more efficient. In the workplace, this could mean that tedious processes such as data entry are done faster and with greater accuracy. AI could also be used to monitor performance metrics and alert employers when something needs attention.

AI can also be used for more sophisticated tasks such as diagnosing illnesses or navigating traffic conditions in real-time. This can lead to improved healthcare outcomes and smoother commutes for everyone involved.

AI can also make services more accessible by providing users with personalized experiences tailored to their individual needs. This could include providing recommendations on products or services based on past history or offering language translation services in real-time.

Overall, by 2030 we can expect AI to provide us with greater convenience and improved access to services that would otherwise not be available. It will also reduce manual labor and help create a future of automation where work is done faster with fewer errors. Finally, AI has the potential to revolutionize how we interact with our environment and provide us with an unprecedented level of control over our lives.

10.5 INTERSECTION BETWEEN HUMAN AND MACHINE LEARNING BY 2030

The intersection between human and machine learning AI in the year 2030 is an exciting prospect. With advances in artificial intelligence, machines will continue to become smarter, faster and more efficient. This will allow machines to take on more complex tasks and work alongside humans in a variety of industries.

At the same time, humans will still remain essential for the development of AI technology. As machines become increasingly sophisticated, humans will be required to provide higher levels of supervision and guidance to ensure that the technology is being used in a safe and responsible manner. In addition, human creativity and problem-solving skills will be essential for developing innovative applications for AI technologies.

The combination of human and machine learning AI could create a number of advantages for businesses around the world such as improved customer service, increased productivity, cost savings, improved safety standards, enhanced security measures and better decision making processes in various industries.

By 2030 we can expect to see AI playing an integral role in almost every industry from healthcare to transportation and beyond. The potential benefits are immense but they must also come with appropriate safeguards against misuse or abuse of this powerful technology. Ultimately it will be up to us as humans to ensure that this intersection between human ingenuity and machine capability is beneficial for everyone involved.

By 2030, Artificial Intelligence will likely become an integral part of our daily lives and it is essential that we take the necessary steps now to ensure its use remains ethical, responsible and inclusive.

intersection between human and machine learning and is designed to help you understand and navigate the ethical considerations of AI.

This sub chapter help you to explore the ethical considerations of AI. As a Startup owner you can integrate or understand how you can approach to your AI product ethically.

Understand The Ethical Considerations Of AI

AI presents several ethical considerations for society, including privacy and surveillance, bias and discrimination, and lack of transparency. Privacy and data protection are not the same thing; AI systems must adhere to laws and regulations as well as being technically robust in order to protect people's privacy. Additionally, AI must be grounded in fundamental rights, societal values, and explain ability to ensure that when AI systems go awry, teams can trace through a complex chain of decisions. As AI becomes increasingly prevalent in our lives, it is important to consider the ethical implications of its use.

Discuss The Implications Of AI On Society

AI has the potential to revolutionize society and the economy, transforming how people work and live. AI can take on repetitive or dangerous tasks, allowing humans to focus on more creative and meaningful work. However, AI also has the potential to reflect societal inequalities, as it is only as unbiased as its creators. Additionally, AI technology can provide unprecedented access to healthcare and other services, but it could also lead to job losses if not regulated properly. Finally, AI can help automate processes and increase efficiency in many industries, but it could also cause privacy issues if not implemented carefully. It is important that policymakers consider all of these implications when designing regulations and guidelines for the use of AI in society.

Develop Strategies For Responsible AI Use

Organizations can develop strategies for responsible AI use by creating systems that enable AI and their business to align with their core values. To do this, they should first establish a governance strategy and shape key objectives, then create responsible AI policies to attract and retain employees with AI skills. They should also develop transparency notes that communicate the intended uses, capabilities, and limitations of their AI applications. Finally, organizations can make responsible AI a company-wide effort by creating a Responsible AI (RAI) Strategy and Implementation (S&I) Pathway. This pathway should include guidelines for designing, developing, testing, procuring, deploying, and using AI applications.

In short by 2030, AI is expected to have a major impact on life and society in North American cities. AI technologies will be commonplace and used for marketing, personalizing services, and transforming the workplace. In order to ensure that these changes are beneficial for society, it is important for researchers, institutions and funders to consider ethical and legal issues associated with the use of AI. Minimizing negative impacts on society requires long-term solutions that take into account both technological advancements and societal needs. With thoughtful planning and implementation, AI can be used to create a better world in the future.

FOLLOW ALONG THE JOURNEY

This book is perfect for you if you have a desire to learn about AI Product Design and Development. You will definitely enjoy this material. In this book author covered all the important topics in detail and with the help of diagrams and charts for better understanding.

I want to add some of early book reader reviews:

"I really enjoyed the book; it was very interesting to read. Although there were a few big differences in opinions of people involved in the different stages of creating a AI (Hardware and Software) product that would be used by the end customer, I felt that it was well rounded and focused on the users and their needs rather than looking at the product from an inanimate data driven point of view."

"This book is a treasure for software entrepreneurs who want to build successful AI software products. The book covers an entire product life cycle, from idea generation to product launch and everything in between. The author covered a wide spectrum of topics, from lean approaches to technology alternatives that could be used to design software products. If you are interested in any aspect of AI software product design or development and you are planning to venture into the market, this book is essential reading."

Before I finish reading this book! Let us make some notes to follow

Why do we Need AI Startups?

What are the Different Stages Of New AI Product Development Process?

How to Creation AI Product Idea With A Product Roadmap?

How to do the AI Product Feasibility study?

How to Analyze and Research your Product Idea?

How to do the Research Of Product Viability In The Market?

How to turn a Idea To A AI Product In The Most Efficient, Speedy And Cost-effective Way   ?

What I need to know about Lean Project Management?

What I need to know Building A Proof-of-concept Design For Required Prototype   ?

What I need to know about Enhance Existing Product For Market Fit?

What I need to know about diamond framework In Product Development?

How To Avoid Software Development AI Startups Failures?

What are the AI startup challenges I might face ?

How much do I know about AI Laws and privacy concerns?

_____

_____

_____

My AI product idea and top 10 take-away from this book

_____

_____

_____

_____

_____

_____

_____

_____

_____

_____

_____

_____

_____

_____

_____

_____

_____

_____

_____

_____

_____

_____

_____

_____

_____

_____

_____

ABOUT THE AUTHOR

Dr. Padmaraj Nidagundi, the author of many technical books, works as an engineer in software development company, also ex AI startup owner, among other works, lives in Latvia, Riga, with his wife and their one child.

In this book, the author's goal is to bring the best technical life experiences lessons.

Author collected his own work experience as a book and took several different AI startups and AI engineer feedback to make this book outstanding. Author wish is that readers of this book grow themselves as a AI startup owner in the tech industry.

Printed in Great Britain
by Amazon

39878858R00099